Why this book may be what you are searching for.

Darla's book goes to the heart of my issues, dealing with the hardest questions such as, "where is my loved one now? does he hear me? does he know how I'm feeling? is he okay? will he be forgiven? has he found peace? is he with family members who will embrace and love him?" Just to know there are others who have experienced the suicide of a precious child and that there are answers out there has helped me so very much. The saving power of the Gospel of Jesus Christ that Darla reminds me of makes it possible for me to bear this experience of losing my son to suicide.

–Nancy Hearn

ooo

This is such a poignant story. The healing balm of these words makes you believe, understand, and embrace the Atonement . . . I felt the tender softness of broken heart and spirit. I felt Darla's love and longing for her son, and felt her reaching out to find, not his, but the Savior's hand.

—Brenda Floyd

ooo

This book is a road map to recovery to help those who have lost a loved one to suicide. The principles are clearly and sensitively written with an inviting personal touch. The process of Darla Isackson's shared journey from despair to joy can help anyone who has experienced the scars of a deep personal trauma to rebuild a meaningful life.

—Gary & Joy Lundberg

ooo

Darla sang my life with her words. Even the details were my experience. I kept bowing my head to say little prayers during the reading. This book is greatly needed and addresses many questions for those left behind.

—Phyllis Gunderson

ooo

As I read this book, I felt as though Darla had taken her soul and wrung it out as a gift of love.

—Patricia Potts

Darla's book contains the most gloriously hopeful message I have ever read! It has taken away all my fears concerning my lost children. It has bridged the gap in my understanding.

—**Tiffany McCray**

ooo

This is the most healing, uplifting book I have read in over a decade. And it is not just for those who have lost loved ones to suicide. It is also tremendously helpful to loved ones of those who have gone astray, have addictions or undiagnosed mental dysfunctions that damage their lives and break our hearts. How can we forgive them? How can God forgive them? How can we live with their choices? How can we be happy again? Darla's book gives hope through gentle reason, scripture and many anecdotes.

—**Lorie Davis**

ooo

Darla answers questions like, "why did a loving God allow this? where is the balance between justice and mercy? is there hope for those who have taken their lives? will I ever feel joy again?" and more. Her thoughtful research, capacity for articulating poignantly and authentically, and her prayerful turning to God will bless all who read her experiences, insights, and story of hope.

–**Karen Trifiletti**

ooo

What a beautiful gift this book is! A true work of the heart. I was only planning to read one chapter a night, but I couldn't stop. Darla creates such intimacy with the reader through honesty and caring. Through her words I felt every rock on this difficult path, and yet each one led me to a greater capacity for joy. Her gentleness and clarity combine to make a beautiful, tender and sensitive body of writing. I feel as if I'm reading the words of a dear friend. What a comfort this book will be for so many people.

—**Ann Campanella**

ooo

I loved After My Son's Suicide! It gives hope and insight into the Atonement and reminds me of the scripture, "a light on the hill." It inspires others to know about God's goodness and mercy and love!

—**Celeste Tipiani**

After my Son's Suicide

After my, Son's Suicide

An LDS Mother Finds Comfort in Christ and Strength to Go On

Darla Isackson

Bitterroot Mountain
PUBLISHING, LLC.

After My Son's Suicide
An LDS Mother Finds Comfort in Christ and Strength to Go On

Copyright © 2010 by Darla Isackson
Bitterroot Mountain Publishing

For use of larger segments, or to have segments sent electronically, contact the author at:
Darla2@xmission.*com*

Website: darlaisackson.*com*

All opinions expressed herein are the author's alone. *This publication is neither sponsored nor endorsed by The Church of Jesus Christ of Latter-day Saints.*

Page Layout and Design by Rob Davis
Cover Design by Rob Davis
Final editing and proofreading by Debbie Bake

ISBN number 978-0-9817874-3-5

Printed in the United States of America
First Printing July 2010
Second Printing December 2010
Third Printing July 2016

Dedicated

to all who have lost a loved one to suicide,
and to my son Brian whose life and death
taught me so much.

May this book partially fulfill my baptismal promise to

"mourn with those that mourn; yea,
and comfort those that stand in need of comfort."

Mosiah 18:9

Acknowledgments

Thank you, Doug, for sticking by me through the good times and the bad. Your steadiness, loyalty and love keep me going. Thanks to my sons, stepsons, and daughters-in-law for all you continue to teach me, and to my grandchildren for the silver song of joy you sing in my life. Thanks, Scott, for double-checking scriptures!

Thank you, Arlene, for being a true sister and friend. Your compassion and good heart and belief in me are gifts from heaven. The Lord knew just the kind of sister I would need. Thank you, Patricia, for being my best cheerleader and most constant source of encouragement. You are the friend every woman should be lucky enough to have.

Thank you, Brenda, for your concern for me, a fellow sufferer. For all these years, every time I've received an e-mail from you I've felt lifted up, cared about, and understood. Your support, feedback, and quotes helped make this book happen. Thanks to other grievers who have given me helpful feedback and encouragement: Bonnie, I needed the assurance that what I was writing could make a difference, and you were so good at giving it. Jenny, you found two quotes that made so much difference! Phyllis, April, Charn, Dee, Carolyn, Ann, Sheri, thanks to all of you.

Thanks to Joy and Gary and to Mary, Pat, Sheila, and Joyce for advice and inspiration. Thank you, Debbie, for adding just the expertise and love that was needed in finalizing the book. For nearly three decades you've added light to my life. You are amazing! Thanks, Rob, for your encouragement and incredible design. People like you make the world a better place.

Thank you, Nancy, for your calming voice and inspiring Christ-centered words on the "Healing Journey" CD. I keep finding comfort, peace, and the ability to relax and sleep that I never could have without it. I'm hoping to share those blessings with my readers.

Thank you Brian, Mom, Dad, and others in the spirit world who inspire and influence me.

Thank you, dear Savior, for Thy Atonement and undying love for us all. I hope this book will extend Thy comfort to many who are hurting. Thank you, Father in Heaven, for never leaving me, and for giving my heart a voice.

Table of Contents

As We Begin
Our Journey Together

The death of a loved one by illness, accident, or old age can be one of life's hardest tests. Added to the grief attending any death, the tragedy of losing a loved one to suicide can threaten identity, self-worth, and even spiritual sanity.

In the years after my son's death, how I wished for a book from a faithful LDS parent who had triumphed over such a loss and could empathize, reassure me that I'd make it, and lead me through the doctrinal dilemmas. As unique as each suicide may be, we all seem to have the need to identify with others who have been through similar adversity. We want to know that someone has experienced this awful sorrow and survived—and that maybe *we* will too.

First-person stories in the general market were helpful but didn't begin to touch the soul-deep questions in my Mormon mind. There are huge issues to be dealt with for those of us whose primary goals are to rear righteous children and have a forever family. What do we do with the ashes of that ideal? The tragedy of Brian's suicide affected me spiritually, emotionally, mentally, and physically. Consequently, this book contains the best answers I've found in each of those areas. I have written what I wish I could have read. I speak not as an authority, but as a mother who also happens to be a writer.

There's no need to read the book from front to back or to read every word. Feel free to check the Table of Contents and turn to the pages that focus on what is most relevant or troubling to you right now. For instance, the "How-to's" and writing exercises that come later may feel like what you need *now* rather than the answers to spiritual questions that come first in the book.

I have poured out my heart on these pages, shared my deepest, truest feelings and some of the most tender and spiritual experiences of my life. I have documented my journey from despair to understanding and hope. One of life's sweetest discoveries can be when sorrow and adversity lead us to a closer relationship with the Savior—when darkness gives way to life's brightest sunrises. In Alma 28:14 we read, "And thus we see the great reason of sorrow, and also of rejoicing—sorrow because of death and destruction among men, and joy because of the light of Christ unto life." I hold out my hand and say, "You too can travel this path filled with the light of Christ unto life."

Note: In common vernacular, the term "survivor" is often used to denote loved ones left behind after a suicide. For instance, I have referred to a website called SOS, which means Survivors of Suicide. However, this term can be confusing to some who first think of "survivor" as one who attempts suicide but survives. For this reason, I have chosen to use the term "suicide griever" or just "griever" most of the time. Keep in mind that both "griever" and "survivor" refer to the family, friends, and others (co-workers, neighbors, etc.) affected by the suicide.

My Story

My eyes locked with his in a strange and joyous sense of reunion the night Brian, my second child, was born. My first experience of delivering a child had been long and hard. In contrast, Brian came so fast the doctor barely made it. Since I had no anesthetic, I was totally alert and able to experience the miracle of Brian's birth in a deep way. I felt a special bond with him from the first.

By the time Brian was eight, I was the mother of five sons and sometimes felt so overwhelmed and exhausted I ran to my bedroom to cry. Brian was the one who would follow me, pat me, and say, "What's the matter, Mommy?" He's also the one who broke my heart.

The week Brian turned sixteen, after attending church all his life, he simply announced he was not going back. By then, he had been drawn into the drug scene. I was beginning to see signs, such as decreased interest in school and sullen behavior. My formerly affectionate and kind son was suddenly rude, even to me. One day after he snapped at me, I put my arms around him and said, "I love you, and I never talk to you like that, so please don't talk that way to me again." He didn't, but he continued to close himself off from all of us.

As soon as I had verification that drugs were involved, that his sullen withdrawal was not just normal teen-age moodiness, I took Brian to the best rehab program I knew about. He insisted that since he was using marijuana only, he could stop by himself, and he did, submitting to monthly drug testing to verify the fact. After his high school graduation he went to Marine boot camp, which he hated. A knee injury gave him a welcome medical release. After his return, he lived on his own and withdrew even further from his family. Thankfully, I always knew where he lived.

Brian was twenty-six when I learned he had been suffering from major depression since the onset of puberty. Here's how my eyes were opened to that fact: After years of refusing all but minimal contact, in February of 1997, out of the blue he called me. I cried with joy when he apologized for shutting us out, and then invited me to come to his apartment. I dropped everything and jumped into my car. Twenty minutes later I was knocking on his door.

We held each other and cried. A window opened and we communicated heart-to-heart. He told me he had recently walked away from two jobs and was suicidal. He was willing to move back home with us and get help. As we continued to talk, he told me he had first tried to kill himself when he was fifteen. Nothing could have shocked me more. It broke my heart that I had been so clueless, utterly unaware of the mental illness that had been causing such deep pain in my child's soul.

My second husband, Doug, barely knew Brian because Brian had joined the Marines about the time of my remarriage and had never lived with us. However, in Brian's time of need, Doug showed great compassion by moving his office out of a downstairs bedroom so Brian could move in. (My elderly mother was living in our upstairs guest room and another grown son in the downstairs bedroom.) We faced an uncertain future together.

The day after Brian was settled in, my mind was a confused mess. Accepting the reality of his early suicide attempt and his current struggle required a total realignment of my perceptions. I developed a raging headache and had to go lie down. Brian brought a chair and sat at the foot of the bed. He was trained in sports massage and he massaged my feet and spoke reassuring words. It seemed like a miracle; for years I had yearned to minister to this prodigal son, and here he was ministering to me. Looking back, I am even more amazed at this kindness considering the mental state he was in.

In the months that followed, I was so grateful to get to know Brian as an adult and to recognize that the traits I had loved in him when he was a child were still there. After a year of counseling and staying drug free, Brian got his Real Estate license and moved out on his own again. He seemed to be coping well and I assumed he was okay, but the next few years were an emotional roller coaster ride. So many times my high hopes for him were dashed. None of his career goals or romances seemed to turn out right. Was he caught up in substance abuse again? What could I do to help? How I wished I could "make everything all better" for him.

The morning of September 27, 2004, dawned bright and clear. I went about my chores little guessing that the day would bring me greater sorrow than I had ever known. Just before noon, three plainclothes members of the police department appeared at my door to bring me the news that Brian, age thirty-three, was dead—by his own hand. Sometime during the night he had slit his wrists and bled to death in the bathtub. His roommate had discovered him in the morning.

How does one assimilate such news? How can a mother's heart bear such anguish? How many tears can one person cry and not dry up or wither into nothingness? I found myself sobbing out not only my current sorrow, but also the grief of nearly two decades of hard experiences with Brian.

Within hours the house was flooded with family, neighbors, and church friends. There was so much to do and so many decisions to make. Kind people dropped everything and came to my aid. Love in action: that's what I would call the outpouring of concern and help I received after my son died. It was a good thing because my mind was refusing to function, screaming out in disbelief, simply not wanting to accept the horrible reality of having to make funeral arrangements for my son.

That night I wrote in my journal:

After everyone left, Doug [my husband] spoke reassuring words to me. We prayed together and he assured me that Brian was with Jesus. Oh, I want to know that! I want Brian to feel loved; I want him to be reassured of his worth and comforted from all the terrible pain he has experienced.

Is it possible for faith to suddenly blossom when a person dies and can no longer doubt the reality of a life after this one because he is living it? Years ago Brian told me he didn't believe in religion anymore. Is my faith sufficient for us both? Do you get to see the Savior when you die if you had quit believing in Him in life?

Were my mom and dad allowed to fold Brian in their loving arms and comfort him? Oh God, don't let Brian be alone and sad; don't let his soul be tormented; don't let his mental anguish, confusion, and emotional pain continue. Dear Father in Heaven, please comfort my son. I know he is Your son too. Let him know he is safe and loved in a boundless and wonderful way. Let him know he matters, his strengths count, and that he can yet prevail.

I paced the floor for hours, wondering, praying: "Oh Lord, please hold and comfort Brian. You love him even more than I do. The only thing I would do right now if I could be with him is take him in my arms, comfort and love him. Oh surely, surely, Your love would be greater for him than mine. Don't reject him. Only You can understand how he could do what he did. But oh, dear God, please forgive him and help him."

The next day I was able to cry with the roommate who had found Brian's body. In former days I would have been uncomfortable with this man who reeked of tobacco and had dark circles under his eyes. But I looked into his kind, hurting eyes and knew he was a gentle, Brian-type person. I loved him instantly and was so grateful for the support he and his family offered in the next few days.

Later, we picked the plot where Brian would be buried in the cemetery closest to our home. That section of the graveyard is labeled "Revelation." I wrote in my journal:

Oh, how I hope to receive "revelation" about this situation and Brian's well-being. Is he all right? My first concern is for the welfare of his soul. What will become of him? Where is he now? There is nothing left to do except trust God with him and pray for him. My heart is so heavy. Will I ever be able to smile again? I have never experienced anything so like a knife in my heart. The pain is so great I wonder how I can bear it. Sometimes I can hardly breathe. And yet I do feel some kind of spiritual power sustaining me.

I love my son with all my heart and can only stand up under the realities of his death because I believe in the hereafter and in the grace, love, and mercy of Christ. I choose faith now, not because I have any unusual spiritual strength but because the alternative is unbearable, and because I've received so many spiritual assurances. I am weak, but God is strong. I can't imagine surviving such sorrow if I didn't wholeheartedly believe in Jesus and His teachings and sense the reality of the Comforter as my Guide.

I've been one of the walking wounded. Since you are reading this book, you may relate. I used to feel like my heart was literally bleeding. In those first few days after Brian's death, only the Comforter gave me the strength to keep going throughout the arrangements, the viewing, the services, and the burial, even when I thought it was impossible to do so. Praying, writing, talking, crying, and being real in the situation was all I could do.

In the months and years that followed, I found myself on a spiritual journey, the depths of which I had never before experienced. It has been the most difficult time of my life, yet in some ways, the most beneficial. No more surfacey skimming of the teachings of Jesus. No more floating along with only casual attention to spiritual things. It had been easy to trust the strength of my "rope of faith" when it was laying coiled at my feet, but now I was dangling by that rope over a precipice. All who live with the reality of the suicide of a loved one are familiar with that precipice.

In the aftermath of suicide, I've felt that my life depended on gaining understanding and finding a more solid, sustaining faith. Never have I had greater motivation spiritually. Join me in my journey; I'll share my own experiences as well as the experiences of others. You and I will explore some of the best scriptures, references, quotes, and resources available with a focus on the teachings of Jesus Christ. Most importantly, we'll invite the Comforter to calm and mend our broken hearts.

The Looming Question: Where Are They Now?

For I am persuaded, that neither death, nor life, nor angels, nor principalities, nor powers, nor things present, nor things to come,

Nor height, nor depth, nor any other creature, shall be able to separate us from the love of God, which is in Christ Jesus our Lord.

Romans 8:38-39

Clinging to Hope

Doth he cry unto any, saying: Depart from me?
Behold, I say unto you, Nay; but he saith:
Come unto me all ye ends of the earth.

2 Nephi 26:25

The utter finality of suicide feels devastating. Once it has happened, it is irreversible and we have to deal with it. When our lives are flattened by this earthquake of suicide, we need all the hope we can find . . . especially because the aftershocks can go on and on, shaking our faith and leaving us with so many unanswered questions and concern for our loved.

Why Didn't God Prevent This from Happening?

Accepting the death of a loved one by illness, accident, or old age is never easy. For me, losing my son to suicide called into question every belief I'd ever had, every assumption I'd ever made.

The first challenge to faith most of us face after the suicide of a loved one is why an all-powerful God lets such things happen. Robynn, whose son, Rustin, hung himself at the tender age of ten, told me of her experience after her son died: "I was in shock! I didn't eat for days. I was confused and exhausted, and I would pray for hours to find some sense in the whole situation. I questioned everything I believed in—every lesson I had ever learned about God and heaven."

This is a common pattern when a person is trying to make sense of a tragedy that makes no sense. No one needs to feel alone in questioning; we all do it. But when we live our lives in the framework given us by the gospel of Jesus Christ and when we have the Holy Ghost to lead us to truth, prayerful searching can bring some semblance of understanding along with ever-increasing hope.

So Much Hope to Share

The greatest hope I want to share is that this life is only a moment in eternity and that God does His full work through Christ in the long-term, not just during this earth life. He is a God of redemption with the power to overcome all worldly maladies as well as the cunning traps of Satan. No matter how long it takes a person to respond, here or hereafter, He keeps reaching out. *Our hope grows as we sense the reality that God is not the author of our suffering, but of our help.*

Voting Again for Agency

Part of that help for me has been the realization that renewing my pre-mortal vote in favor of agency is a requirement for coming to any place of peace. When I voted for agency the first time, I knew that God's plan of absolute freedom of choice would bring grief. I knew then that God's agency would not be "selective," that He would not step in and stop every grievous choice so all those involved could avoid pain. Satan convinced 1/3 of our spirit siblings that he could stop all wrong choices and stop the inevitable pain and suffering that would result from unfettered agency. But those of us who chose Christ and His plan knew there was no better way—that only the hard lessons learned from choice and consequences could prepare us to become like God.

It is probable that we also knew about and accepted, in that pre-mortal realm, the risks of living in a world where natural law dictates consequences that are final. For example, a suicide victim can't say the next moment or the next day, "I changed my mind. I want to go back and do it differently." We voted for God's plan there, and in the midst of our current suffering, we can find moments of peace by seconding that vote now.

Remembering that God is the author of our help, let me share now the incredible help He gave me as I struggled to understand and come to peace with Brian's state in the spirit world.

Concern for the Loved One

I had so many questions, so few answers. But the purpose of this book is to share the answers I have found in the intervening years.

Another mother dealing with her son's suicide e-mailed me with her fear concerning the condition of her son's soul. She said, "Dealing with the fact that he took his own life is the most unbearable part—not that he is gone, not that he passed to another stage of his life, but that he took his own life to get there. Because of that I worry about the outcome."

Concern for Brian continued to be foremost in my mind in the days and weeks that followed.

The Aching Question of Sin

As much as I wanted to hide from the fact, I knew that suicide—taking one's own life—is a serious sin. In the shadowy nights that followed Brian's death I sobbed for assurance that Brian was surrounded by the Savior's love. I had heard that suicide is akin to murder, and is unforgivable. Was Brian lost forever? I knew his heart and simply couldn't believe that. I began to read every article, book, and scripture I could find that might clarify the Church's teachings on suicide.

Because so many struggle with this heart-wrenching issue, and because all other issues have seemed secondary in importance, I want to deal with it first. Oh how relieved I was to find *nothing* in the scriptures or words of the apostles and prophets to verify the idea that our loved ones can't repent of the sin of suicide—or other sins they may have been caught up in at the time of their death.

I'm not ignoring what Alma said about not procrastinating the day of our repentance, but sometimes that scripture is taken out of context. I want to show you a larger picture. Digressing from my story for a while, I'm going to share some of the many evidences I've found that repentance and forgiveness continue in the spirit world.

I bear my witness that God is a God of mercy; the Savior stretches out His loving arms, offering forgiveness to the truly repentant, here *and* hereafter. He takes into consideration every detail of a person's heart, intentions, and circumstance—which He alone knows. And we have every assurance that suicide itself is not an unpardonable sin.

Just the other day I thought of a Book of Mormon passage that shows, depending on circumstances, that even multiple murders are forgivable. Consider the Anti-Nephi-Lehies who gave this touching account:

> *And I also thank my God, yea, my great god, that he hath granted unto us that we might repent of these things, and also that he hath forgiven us of those our many sins and murders which we have committed, and taken away the guilt from our hearts, through the merits of his Son. (Alma 24:10)*

You might feel some fear that this doesn't apply beyond the veil, but oh, I hope you will withhold judgment until you have read the first two chapters of this book. I'm sure you will see that it does.

Let's start with Elder Boyd K. Packer's landmark address titled "The Brilliant Morning of Forgiveness."[1] Elder Packer clearly states that the Lord's servants continue the work of redemption beyond the veil—and that, except for the few who defect to perdition, no sin is exempt from the promise of complete forgiveness through the Atonement of Christ. That means the Lord will remember the sin no more! If you have any question whatsoever whether suicide can be forgiven, read this talk!

In the October 2009 General Conference, Elder Neil L. Andersen gave the same reassurance that, except for the sins of those few who choose perdition after having known a fulness, there is no sin that cannot be forgiven.[2]

I know that redemption and forgiveness do not assure exaltation, but still, there is great hope.

The Savior Stretches Wide His Arms

I recently re-read the story of the Prodigal Son and was struck by these words: "When he [the son] was a yet a great way off, his father saw him, and had compassion, and ran, and fell on his neck, and kissed him" (Luke 15:20). That father clearly symbolizes our Heavenly Father. He is full of love for even His prodigal children.

The most common feeling expressed by those who have been on the other side is that they were loved beyond comprehension. We are told that "the spirits of all men, as soon as they are departed from this mortal body, yea, the spirits of all men, whether they be good or evil, are taken home to that God who gave them life" (Alma 40:11). And when He takes them home they are surely greeted with a greater love than we can even imagine.

We know that death does not sweep away accountability or shield a person from the consequences of actions or the sorrow for sin necessary for repentance. However, we can still have a perfect brightness of hope for the ultimate salvation of our loved ones. I've documented good reasons for that hope in this chapter and the next.

Comforting Words from an Apostle of the Lord

A daughter-in-law, Traci, brought us a booklet called *Suicide: Some Things We Know, and Some We Do Not,* by Elder M. Russell Ballard.[3] In it we found many answers and a measure of comfort for our aching hearts. If you have not already seen it, I recommend that you immediately look it up on lds.org in the *Ensign* archives or obtain a copy from Deseret Book. It is instructive and helpful and calmed many of our fears.

Elder Ballard's major point is that even though suicide is a sin, only the Lord knows a person's heart and circumstances; only He can judge—and He will do so mercifully. He quotes the Prophet Joseph Smith:

While one portion of the human race is judging and condemning the other without mercy, the Great Parent of the universe looks upon the whole of the human family with a fatherly care and paternal regard

... He is a wise Lawgiver, and will judge all men, not according to the narrow, contracted notions of men.[4]

Elder Ballard also quoted from President Joseph F. Smith's vision of the redemption of the dead (D&C 138:57-59), parts of which I quote in the next chapter. He concluded with gratitude for the plan of salvation, a plan of fairness and love. He reminded those experiencing the agony of a loved one's suicide of the Lord's promise and blessing: "Peace I leave with you, my peace I give unto you: not as the world giveth, give I unto you. Let not your heart be troubled, neither let it be afraid" (John 14:27).

Another Voice of Hope

As time went by, even though I was finding great comfort, the sadness of Brian's death—and of his life—plagued me. I wondered why his every effort (and he made many) to establish himself in a career had turned to dust, why he seemed to live his whole adult life under a black cloud of "bad luck." I found myself recounting an incredibly long list of things that had gone wrong for him and wondering how anyone could have held up under that onslaught year after year.

I wondered why some people are born into situations where they seem to receive every opportunity and advantage for the development and use of their talents, and others seem to get so little. I admitted to myself that in Brian's case he had turned his back on help from family for many years and much of his "bad luck" resulted from poor decisions. But why are some blessed with sound minds and others plagued their whole life with mental illness? Brian was struggling with a full-blown mental illness by the time he was fifteen! I grieved at how difficult my son's life had been in spite of his intelligence, talent, and a spirit that I knew to be good.

Then I was given the account of a faithful member of the Church, Brother Larry St. Clair. As a former home teacher and friend of the family, he was asked to speak at the funeral of a teenager named David. David had lived a tragic life of deprivation, abuse, and poor choices and had finally taken his own life. Brother St. Clair had never dealt with the suicide issue before and had no idea what to say. He prayed with his whole soul for direction, but none seemed to come. Finally, during the prelude music for the funeral he was given a vision of David in the arms of Christ. In the vision, the Savior looked at Brother St. Clair and said: "My son David is all right now. I love him and I will heal and make him whole again. You must not worry about David any longer; no one can cause him pain or grief ever again."

Clearly inspired now with what the Lord wanted him to say, he explained to those gathered that the unfairness, unkindness and tragedy of David's life had been completely swallowed up through the power of Christ's Atonement. Brother St. Clair explained: "I now knew that, in the final analysis, a significant portion of the Atonement of Jesus Christ was dedicated to compensating for the unwarranted bitterness of mortality. I take great hope from the fact that I now know that the Davids of this world will ultimately be loved and healed and made whole again through the infinite goodness and love of the Master Himself. And for the first time in my life I understood how very, very much Christ loved *me*."

I bear witness of that love for each of us. We have been dear to Him since the beginning of time and His whole desire is to strengthen, comfort, and cleanse us—here and hereafter.

Why We Should Continue to Choose Life

I was asked by one troubled reader, "Well, if things are so wonderful on the other side, why should we stay in this vale of tears?" I have felt between a rock and a hard place in choosing what to include in this book. So many stories like Larry St. Clair's, so many scriptures and words of the prophets offer the most incredible picture of hope, but I don't want to say anything that could be mistaken as motivation or justification to a person who is sitting on the edge, wanting to join a departed loved one. Families of those who die by suicide may be at greater risk than others because of the ripple effect. We can and must fortify ourselves and our families against it.

Every person needs to be aware of the risks and the patterns. Resources for suicide prevention abound, such as The American Foundation for Suicide Prevention. Check out their website: http://www.afsp.org/ which offers excellent help and guidelines for survivors as well as anyone who is struggling with suicidal thoughts and feelings.

So, even though this book has not been written for the suicidal, but for grievers, I need to make clear the following: *The Lord desires that we "fight the good fight, finish our course, keep the faith."* (See 2 Timothy 4:7.) Opportunities abound to learn and to serve—even up to the last breath, which the Lord in His wisdom lends us. I still remember the powerful message of a story I read in a college English class nearly fifty years ago: less than an hour after his failed suicide attempt, a man saved another person's life. The point was poignantly made that each moment of life is precious and His will is that we *embrace life* until God in His great wisdom takes us home.

The biggest lie the adversary whispers to suicidal individuals is that the whole world would be better off without them. But each of us plays a unique part in the unfolding of God's purposes and is needed here more than we could ever imagine. To dwell on the peace and love and comfort available in the spirit world without perspective can increase the ripple effect. One mother confided that she is almost certain her son made a decision to follow his Young Men's leader in suicide when he attended the leader's funeral and the whole focus of the talks centered on the idea that "now, at last, he has found the peace he never found in life." She said she watched her troubled son's face and her heart sank. Shortly thereafter her son took his own life in the same way his leader had.

Years ago I edited a book by Joyce Brown called *Heavenly Answers to*

Earthly Questions.[5] Her book included—in her near-death experience—her vision of the spirits of several people who had taken their own lives. Attending the funerals and viewings, Joyce saw the anguish these people felt at the grief they had caused those who loved them. They kept saying, "I'm so sorry, I'm so sorry." They could see the blessings they had thrown away, such as continued opportunities to interact with family and friends on the earth. They were suffering.

I hated thinking about those scenes after Brian died. I have no doubt that he suffered through a time of great sorrow and regret for his suicide. I was appreciative, therefore, of the perspective I received from a mother named Diana. She e-mailed me about her son who took his life, saying, "My impressions are that the 'suffering' he is doing is the suffering we all go through in the repentance process. And that it is accompanied with joy and relief."

How Long Does Repentance Take?

Regardless of the situation, every survivor of a loved one's suicide is left with a multitude of questions. Here's some more I recorded in my journal: "Where is Brian now? Does he know how much we miss him? I don't have a recording of his voice—will I forget how he sounded? What is it like for him over there? Is he still suffering? Was he immediately open to gospel truth or did he resist it as he did so many times here?"

Just weeks after Brian's death I had been reading in Alma (in the Book of Mormon) and afterwards wrote in my journal:

> *I think Alma's words where he is telling his son about his experience are important in regard to the subject of suicide. First, Alma describes his torment: "Oh, thought I, that I could be banished and become extinct both soul and body . . . I was racked with torment" (Alma 36). These words describe as near as I can imagine how a suicidal person feels. Only those who have experienced it can fully understand the depth of the torment.*

11

Here is the hopeful part: Alma, remembering what he had heard of Jesus, though he could not speak or move, cried out in his heart: "O Jesus, thou Son of God, have mercy on me, who am in the gall of bitterness, and am encircled about by the everlasting chains of death. And now, behold, when I thought this, I could remember my pains no more; yea, I was harrowed up by the memory of my sins no more. And oh, what joy, and what marvelous light I did behold; yea, my soul was filled with joy as exceeding as was my pain! Yea, I say unto you, my son, that there could be nothing so exquisite and so bitter as were my pains. Yea, and again I say unto you, my son, that on the other hand, there can be nothing so exquisite and sweet as was my joy."

Surely in his life review Brian would remember the testimonies of Christ he had heard borne during his time on earth, the scriptures he read, the sacrament songs he sang about the love and mercy of Jesus. Surely he would grasp hold of those and cry out to the Savior as Alma did, "O Jesus, thou Son of God, have mercy on me." (See Alma 36.)

As soon as Alma repented and hardened not his heart, *immediately* his pain was gone and he felt the joy of the great plan of redemption. I believe that the Lord does not want us to suffer one minute longer than we need to in order to repent. Repentance means, more than anything, a change of mind and heart—and that repentance does not have to mean long years of internal torment. Suicidal people have already suffered so much! Surely the torment in the spirit world lasts only long enough to motivate a person to reach out to Jesus for relief, and could only be prolonged by a person's refusal to do so. I know the Lord is a merciful God and desires for each of us to take advantage of the Atonement as quickly and fully as we are willing.

The Savior is a Being of light and truth, and knowing the truth can be painful—but the truth also brings profound relief from Satan's lies. I believe Brian now has some vital things he lacked here: hope in Christ, knowledge of how to access the Atonement, and a recognition that he is a precious son of God who is loved beyond measure.

Sources of Help Abound

In the next chapter you will find the most hopeful ideas I've found about the spirit world, documenting why repentance is still possible there. The more I look, the more I find voices of comfort that are healing and welcome. Justice is an eternal principle, but so is mercy. The Atonement makes mercy possible. When the bishop read me the paragraphs about suicide from the Church Handbook of Instructions, I was even more encouraged. You may want to ask your bishop to read them to you.

People who have come back from the brink of suicide often tell of the tempting thoughts in their minds urging them to destroy themselves, assuring them death is the only way to find peace from their unbearable mental torment. Here's what I've come to believe: Satan momentarily wins the battle with those he convinces to take their own lives—often through the illness itself. But he has not won the war! The biggest reason I must share what I've learned about the painful dilemma of suicide is to witness that the Savior's song of redeeming love will reach them still. I have found solid comfort and hope in the truths of the gospel, and you can too.

There is a balm in Gilead, there is comfort, there is hope. I urge you to reach out for it—and to reach out for Him, the final and true source of all hope.

Notes

1. Elder Boyd K. Packer, "The Brilliant Morning of Forgiveness," October 1995 General Conference, *New Era*, Apr. 2005, 4.

2. See Neil L. Andersen, "Repent . . . That I May Heal You," *Ensign*, Nov. 2009, 40-42.

3. His message first appeared in the *Ensign*, Oct. 1987, and since 1993 has been available in booklet form from Deseret Book.

4. *Teachings of the Prophet Joseph Smith,* edited by Joseph Fielding Smith, Salt Lake City, Utah, Deseret Book Co., 1938, 218.

5. Joyce Brown's books, *Heavenly Answers to Earthly Questions* and *Heavenly Answers to Earthly Challenges* are out of print, but used copies are available. Her latest edition is called *Heavenly Answers.*

What Happens in the Spirit World?

They were assembled awaiting the advent
of the Son of God into the spirit world,
to declare their redemption from the bands of death.

D&C 138:16

My yearning to know how Brian was doing and what was happening to him in the spirit world continued. Sometimes I addressed my questions to him in my journal. I wrote, "Oh Brian, where are you now? Are you far away or are you close to us? Are you accepting what you are being taught? What kind of progress are you making there?"

With an insatiable appetite for answers, I continued reading everything I could find on the subject of the spirit world. (In early drafts of this book I included a section of many of the excellent quotes that resulted. However, since it is not possible to get permission to print that many quotes, I offer just a few, along with my conclusions and the best scripture passages and references. Feel free to contact me through my website for more.)

When Does the Second Estate End?

Today I was lying in my backyard hammock, watching summer sunlight filter through the leaves of the trees, pondering the journey I've taken in my quest to understand what happens in the spirit world.

From the time I was a child I heard that missionary work was going on in the spirit world. That knowledge had made me question the idea that "if you don't understand and repent by the time you die it is too late." I started this book with only a tentative hope that our second estate probation continues after death, because "second estate" is usually defined as our time "on this earth." Because it seemed like such a major issue to me, I looked at that from every angle and decided that part of the assurance I was looking for might be in the documentation I'd found that the spirit world *is* "on this earth."

As a robin swooped low over the hammock, then perched in the tree nearest me, I thought of the day I found those quotes. Elder Parley P. Pratt wrote that the spirit world "is here on the very planet where we were born; or in other words, the earth and other planets of like sphere, have their inward or spiritual spheres, as well as their outward, or temporal. The one is peopled by temporal tabernacles and the other by spirits. A veil is drawn between the one sphere and the other, whereby all the objects in the spiritual sphere are rendered invisible to those in the temporal."[1]

Also, Brigham Young spoke extensively about the spirit world and said it is "right here."[2] I was so excited to think of my loved ones being so near. But did that prove anything about the second estate continuing?

Another landmark was finding the article "The Spirit World, Our Next Home," by Dale C. Mouritsen, an area director of seminaries and institutes (a must read). To summarize, he said that the spirit world is a tangible, substantial sphere incorporated with our earth, the focal point of a massive missionary effort.[3]

I concluded that whether we call our time in the spirit world an extension of our second estate or something else, there would be no point of preaching the gospel in the spirit world if those who heard the preaching couldn't benefit from it. We know those in the spirit world are still able to choose to accept or reject the gospel as well as the proxy ordinances we do for them. And that was as far as I had come with the subject when I started this book.

I smiled, climbed out of the hammock, and went into the house. I was eager to get back to my computer because now I could tell you the best part! I had continued to search for verification that the second estate does not end when we die. This was an important issue and I wanted to know for sure! Imagine my delight when Jenny, an e-mail friend and griever, sent me a quote from President Marion G. Romney that specifically said that! In a talk titled "We Are Children of God,"[4] he plainly defines the second estate as *the mortality we are now experiencing AND our sojourn in the spirit after we die.*

But the best was yet to come. (And hearing this you will understand better why I had to keep writing and rewriting this chapter.) During the final stages of creating this book I learned that Elder Neal A. Maxwell, in his book *The Promise of Discipleship*, had written an entire chapter on the spirit world! I obtained a copy of the book and read chapter 9. (It starts on page 105.) Elder Maxwell's words are so full of hope for our departed loved ones! In that chapter called simply "The Spirit World," I found the following quote:

> We tend to overlook the reality that the spirit world and paradise are part, really, of the second estate. The work of the Lord, so far as the second estate is concerned, is completed before the Judgment and the Resurrection . . . He gave us our spirit birth, bringing the first estate to all. He gave the gift to us of mortality, or the second estate, where all might be "added upon" . . . He provides in the spirit world a continuum of mortality's probation, the great opportunity for all.[5]

How could it be any different? God is both merciful and just. What else would make sense? One of my sons got that message early on. On February 18, 2005, I wrote in my journal, "My son Scott said he received a new insight: that we have all the time we need—here and hereafter—to learn what we need to learn." And to change what we need to change!

Joseph F. Smith's Vision of the Redemption of the Dead

For a long time my best comfort had been President Joseph F. Smith's vision of the redemption of the dead in Doctrine & Covenants 138. He said, in part:

> *But behold, from among the righteous, he organized his forces and appointed messengers, clothed with power and authority, and commissioned them to go forth and carry the light of the gospel to them that were in darkness, even to all the spirits of men; and thus was the gospel preached to the dead.*
>
> *And the chosen messengers went forth to declare the acceptable day of the Lord and proclaim liberty to the captives who were bound, even unto all who would repent of their sins and receive the gospel.*
>
> *Thus was the gospel preached to those who had died in their sins, without a knowledge of the truth, or in transgression, having rejected the prophets.*
>
> *These were taught faith in God, repentance from sin, vicarious baptism for the remission of sins, the gift of the Holy Ghost by the laying on of hands,*
>
> *And all other principles of the gospel that were necessary for them to know in order to qualify themselves that they might be judged according to men in the flesh, but live according to God in the Spirit.*
>
> *And so it was made known among the dead, both small and great, the unrighteous as well as the faithful, that redemption had been wrought through the sacrifice of the Son of God upon the cross.*
> (D&C 138:30-35)

The last verses of that section summarize this hopeful doctrine:

> *I beheld that the faithful elders of this dispensation, when they depart from mortal life, continue their labors in the preaching of the gospel of repentance and redemption, through the sacrifice of the Only Begotten Son of God, among those who are in darkness and under the bondage of sin in the great world of the spirits of the dead.*

The dead who repent will be redeemed, through obedience to the ordinances of the house of God.

And after they have paid the penalty of their transgressions, and are washed clean, shall receive a reward according to their works, for they are heirs of salvation.

Thus was the vision of the redemption of the dead revealed to me, and I bear record, and I know that this record is true, through the blessing of our Lord and Savior, Jesus Christ, even so. Amen. (D&C 138:57-60)

The dictionary definition of redemption is, "To free from captivity by payment of ransom." Those who accept the gospel and the Savior *in the spirit world* will be ransomed by the Atonement and freed from their sins. And look at this verse again: "Thus was the gospel preached to those who had died in their sins, without a knowledge of the truth, or in transgression, having rejected the prophets" (D&C 138:32). No matter what was going on in the lives of our loved ones who took their own lives, surely they would be included in that promise. The only purpose for teaching the dead about the mission of the Savior, as Section 138 so clearly says *will be taught*, is that the blessings of the Atonement are extended to them still.

My father was a faithful elder, an untiring missionary all the days of his life. I can easily imagine him joyfully sharing the fullness of the gospel with loved ones who had not understood it in this life. In my mind's eye I can see Brian gladly listening, and saying, "Oh, so that's it!" I can see him rejoicing in the doctrine of the Atonement once he really understood it. I can imagine him willingly paying any price (the penalty of his transgressions, as is mentioned in verse 59) to be able to stand with the righteous.

It's hard for me to imagine anything closer to hell than the condition of mind that prompts suicide. But after they have repented they can proclaim: "Behold, the Lord hath redeemed my soul from hell; I have beheld his glory, and I am encircled about eternally in the arms of his love" (2 Nephi 1:15). Repentance opens the door to redemption.

Evidence That People Repent in the Spirit World

I found more evidence after the book had gone to press, which I am adding to this printing, such as Brent and Wendy Top's book *Glimpses Beyond Death's Door: Gospel Insights into Near-death Experiences.* (See Resource section.) The authors reference many other books that recount or analyze near-death experiences. They clearly state that the gospel blesses us with the understanding that death does not mark the final judgment and that even in the world of spirits opportunities to come unto Christ are afforded to mankind by a merciful, loving, and fair God. They show that many near-death experiences offer compelling evidence to substantiate this belief.

In his superb book, *The Infinite Atonement,* author Tad R. Callister documented the fact that the Atonement reaches back into premortality, then says that the redeeming powers of the Savior reach forward to reach the spirits of the dead just as readily as they stretched back to premortal life.[6] "If in this life only we have hope in Christ, we are of all men most miserable" (1 Corinthians 15:19). Our hope in Christ need never end!

Now that I've resolved so many things in my mind, I don't like to remember how worried I was about Brian at first. Like when I read the scripture, "Ye cannot say, when ye are brought to that awful crisis [referring to death], that I will repent, that I will return to my God. Nay, ye cannot say this; for that same spirit which doth possess your bodies at the time that ye go out of this life, that same spirit will have power to possess your body in that eternal world" (Alma 34:34).

Brian had shown such resistance to anything to do with religion for years; I worried that same spirit would keep him from listening there. But what was his real spirit, his real identity? My youngest son, Scott, was working a night security job at the time of Brian's death. He e-mailed me the following morning: "I've been grieving for Brian during the night, but in the end I feel very uplifted and cheered concerning his state." Scott reminded me of a woman's experience where she was allowed to see the spirit of a man others looked down on. She saw he was a great and noble person—like the spirit we had often felt in Brian in spite of his problems.

Still I wondered, and I wrote in my journal:

Will Brian even listen when he has a chance to hear the gospel in the spirit world? Surely teachers on the other side know far better than I ever have how to share the precious truths of life and salvation. Will my continued prayers for him help open his heart to these truths?

So many quotes gave me hope. President Brigham Young said: "When the spirits leave their bodies they are in the presence of our father and God; they are prepared then to see, hear and understand spiritual things."[7]

That could well explain my temple experience with my husband's great-grandmother, Wendla Sofia Lofsund. She was an anti-Mormon bootlegger with little room in her life for religion. Can you imagine my surprise when, as her proxy, I strongly *felt* her acceptance and her joy as I performed her temple ordinances? I'd never had that happen before—and it happened before Brian died. The experience with Wendla was such a strong evidence that now, years later, I still feel a great spiritual swelling to even write of it. It gives me comfort and hope in regard to my son.

I know that "the dead who repent will be redeemed." I know that Wendla had the gospel preached to her in its purity and power after she died, and that she repented and accepted it. And I know for sure that she accepted her temple work. I was there! What could have given me greater hope for Brian's situation?

Hopeful Words about Conditions in the Spirit World

I'm still pondering quotes that indicate it may be harder to repent in the spirit world than it is here. I believe this applies to certain sins that have to do with the body, but it does not seem to apply to the basic principle of accepting the truth.

My next great find was a talk by President Lorenzo Snow called "Preaching the Gospel in the Spirit World." It is electrifying—definitely on my "most recommended" list to read! He assures us that the success of missionaries in the spirit world far exceeds what we see here, that there are few indeed who do not gladly receive the Gospel, because circumstances there will be a thousand times more favorable.[8]

A thousand times more favorable! Think of what that really means. For one thing, it means that the adversary won't be present whispering distortions and false interpretations or creating resistance to truth. It means that the doctrines of Christ will be presented in absolute purity. So many of Brian's "objections" to religion were based on misunderstandings—the ideas of men mingled with scriptures—along with the hypocrisy he observed. None of that will be present where he is now.

Robert L. Millet wrote:

> *I have a conviction that when a person passes through the veil of death, all those impediments and challenges and crosses that were beyond his or her power to control—abuse, neglect, immoral environment, weighty traditions, etc.—will be torn away like a film. Then perhaps that person shall, as President Woodruff suggested, see and feel things he or she could not see and feel before.*[9]

I believe that in the spirit world, a person's real, true spirit is unmasked. Yes, they take the spirit with them that they possessed here, but underneath the pain and misunderstandings, our loved ones had such beautiful spirits. Most of their problems here may have been the result of emotional or mental illness that made it impossible for them to feel good about themselves. Of course, coupled with that was the adversary's success at deceiving them—convincing them they were so much less than they really were and tempting them to actions that compounded their problems. Basking in the love of the Lord's spirit, I believe that our loved ones in the spirit world are re-learning their identity.

We are talking here about Saturday's Warriors—about youth of the noble birthright, so valiant in the pre-mortal life that they were saved to come forth in the last days, where they were taught the Restored gospel and baptized into Christ's church. Some who die by suicide have been endowed and served missions and married in the temple. The things Alma says about the fate of the evil and wicked—all telestial beings or sons of perdition—simply don't apply to most of our loved ones. (See Alma 34:33-35; Alma 40:13-14.) We don't believe the sectarian doctrine of heaven and hell with its terrible arbitrary line drawn between the two that dictates, "those who commit just one too many sins will be cast out with the wicked." Leaving the Church (or turning away the missionaries) or getting caught up in drugs without understanding what they are doing does not categorize them as "wicked."

These loved ones of ours who have died by suicide are choice people who have been waylaid, detoured, temporarily snared by some combination of mental illness, addiction, and Satan's wiles. I have read that those who are lured into the counterfeit "ups" of substance abuse are often tenderhearted souls chafing under the bleakness of mortality and yearning for life to be more beautiful. They had temporarily forgotten who they were. But we had glimpses of who they are, (think of them as little children) and in a beautiful and complete way God knows who they are.

Here's what the Prophet Joseph Smith said about them:

> *Though some of the sheep may wander, the eye of the Shepherd is upon them, and sooner or later they will feel the tentacles of Divine Providence reaching out after them and drawing them back to the fold. Either in this life or in the life to come, they will return. They will have to pay their debt to justice; they will suffer for their sins; and may tread a thorny path; but if it leads them at last, like the penitent Prodigal, to a loving and forgiving father's heart and home, the painful experience will not have been in vain.*[10]

I love the scripture in Isaiah 1:18, "Come now, and let us reason together, saith the Lord: though your sins be as scarlet, they shall be as white as snow; though they be red like crimson, they shall be as wool." I took all that I know about our merciful God and reasoned it out. Does the Lord's cleansing power continue in the spirit world? Undoubtedly.

Our loved ones in the spirit world still have infinite possibilities. Elder Maxwell continued in the same chapter I mentioned previously:

> *Since those who go to the celestial kingdom include, as revealed,*
> *those who "overcome by faith" (D&C 76:53), the same efforts and tri-*
> *umph would need to occur in the spirit world before they receive resur-*
> *rection and the entitlement to enter the celestial kingdom . . . Again, our*
> *existence in the spirit world is part of the mortal sector of our Father's*
> *plan which culminates with the Judgment and the Resurrection.[11]*

Why don't we hear more about this? My only conclusion is that we, as mortals, are all too likely to procrastinate if we think we have plenty of time—and the sooner we repent, the better. Heaven only knows, we have been given plenty of reasons to make repentance a part of our daily lives. For me personally, knowing more about the spirit world give me greater, not less, motivation to repent now!

Dale C. Mouritsen, in the article previously referred to, also indicated that the more aware we become that the spirit world is a real extension of our mortal existence, the less likely we are to fasten our hearts on the treasures of this world.[12]

I believe that recognition of the great work in progress in the spirit world in behalf of all those who have passed on can be our greatest source of encouragement.

Triumphing Over Our Enemies

Larry Barkdull, in his book *Rescuing Wayward Children*, indicated that redemption comes down to one truth: the Holy Spirit is the key to happiness, and to lack the Holy Spirit is the source of misery. The devil attempts to keep us all in ignorance about this truth. But when the Lord reaches out and blesses our children with this knowledge, whether in this life or the next, salvation is at hand.

I like to imagine Brian turning to Jesus Christ and experiencing the Lord's grace as He helps him triumph over all his enemies and "put them under his feet," never again to be afflicted in this world or in the world to come. Like Paul and Alma, our loved ones will be presented with a merciful option—to forsake their sins, experience redemption, ascend from their fallen state, and help bring others with them. Larry Barkdull says, "This is the pattern, and this, we have good cause to hope, will be their destiny."

The Wonder of the Spirit World

It is clear that our probationary second estate includes the spirit world existence—that our probation is not over until judgment day. We know there are preliminary judgments which correspond with the various times of resurrection. Christ was the first resurrected, and many have been resurrected since. But the final judgment is not until the end of the Millennium, after the last resurrection. The Lord hasn't finished His work until then. (See D&C 76:85.) And what is His work? Redemption is His mighty work which culminates in the resurrection. "And the resurrection from the dead is the redemption of the soul" (D&C 88:16).

My sister listened to a temple sealer answer the question, "If the people we are being sealed for are already dead, why do we seal them for *time* and all eternity? Hasn't the 'time' part already passed for them?" The answer, "Time refers to all that transpires until the end of the Millennium on this earth. Eternity refers to all that transpires after the Millennium."

This is part of the good news of the gospel that impacts not only those who missed out on it during mortality, but for all of us who have the gospel in its fullness but need more time to learn to apply what we know!

And so many people do not have the opportunity to learn eternal truths during mortality. Millions never hear of Christ, never know the true gospel, never experience Christ-like love. Many are never cherished or given a sense of their worth—and certainly never have the opportunity for baptism or temple ordinances by priesthood authority. Many others, like Brian, receive baptism as children, but never understand its importance and wander off before they can gain a deeper understanding of Christ's Atonement.

Only The Church of Jesus Christ of Latter-day Saints holds out the assurance that sacred ordinances will be performed by proxy. Every person ever born will have the opportunity to be taught and *really understand* the gospel. They will choose to accept or reject it, not on the basis of prejudice, emotion, or distorted ideas, but on clear and true understanding.

That process happens in the spirit world for so many millions. They choose there whether to accept or reject spirit world missionaries, whether to accept or not accept proxy temple ordinances. Their decisions still count. They still have the possibility to learn, to progress, and repent.

Sweet Witnesses of the Spirit

I recently re-read my journal entries for the year after Brian died, and was thrilled to note that on two separate occasions I had received a spiritual witness that Brian now knows the gospel truths he resisted here. I love this entry made December 24, 2004, not even three months after he died:

> *I was listening to a tape in* The Work and the Glory *series. Joseph Smith turns to Lydia and begins talking to her about her recently deceased father—who had been so bitter against Joseph, the Church, and the Book of Mormon. He said he suspected that Josiah McBride's opinion might be changed by having the Angel Moroni sit down and chat with him about directing Joseph to the gold plates.*
>
> *I started to cry and the words came to my mind, "Brian knows now. Brian KNOWS." I was filled with peace and hope and assurance that he had been taught in perfect clarity, in a way totally acceptable to him, the reality of the Restoration, the plan of salvation, the mission of the Savior, and how the Atonement applies to him. Nothing could comfort me more.*

But something *did* comfort me even more. A few months later, on June 5, 2005, I recorded the moment when the Holy Ghost told me for sure that Brian not only knew of Christ, but had also *accepted* Him.

> *Had a special study time with scriptures in the morning and was left with a burning desire to know if Brian is accepting the gospel and feeling*

what I am feeling, is knowing the truth of God and the redeeming power
of Christ. Went into the kitchen to get a drink of water and the Spirit
washed over me and I KNEW, I KNEW Brian has chosen Christ, is re-
penting and making great progress. I can't begin to express the joy this
brings me. There is absolutely nothing I have desired more than to know
that Brian has accepted the love and teachings of Jesus.

Nothing surpasses the "knowing" in our hearts that comes from the
Holy Ghost. The Savior is a Being of light and truth; truth conveyed by the
Spirit brings profound relief from Satan's lies. Such experiences are part of
my personal witness to you. Quotes from church leaders are wonderful, but
the best witness of all is from the Holy Ghost. I've received that witness and
it is available to you too. As members of the Church we have been given the
Gift of the Holy Ghost—the Spirit of Truth.

So many things I may not know until I enter the spirit world myself.
But so many things I know for sure right now because the Holy Ghost has
borne witness to my soul: that God lives, that the spirit world is real, and
that the Lord sends angels to escort dear ones when they leave this life. That
last one I know from a special witness of the Spirit in regard to my mother's
death (which occurred four years before Brian's). Here's a brief summary of
the experience:

Three weeks before my elderly mother died in my home, I went into
her room at 7:00 a.m. and she was wide awake, her face glowing—
which was a drastic change because she had been very depressed.
She told me there had been angels in her room and one said to the
other, "Look at Fern. She's almost ready. We'll come and get her in
three weeks." Our home was filled with light and love, and three weeks
later—to the hour—my mother took her last breath and passed peace-
fully to the other side.

I've never had a sweeter experience than being in the same room
where angels had been. As strange as it may seem, I felt that same sense of

sweetness and peace (instead of the terror I expected) when I entered the room where Brian died. My heart knew that angels had been there. My heart knows he's with angels now—and that he is one of them!

Notes

1. Parley P. Pratt, *Key to the Science of Theology,* 9th ed., Deseret Book, 1965, 126–27.

2. *Journal of Discourses,* 3:368-69.

3. Dale C. Mouritsen, "The Spirit World, Our Next Home," *Ensign,* Jan. 1977, 47.

4. Marion G. Romney, "We Are Children of God," *Ensign,* Sept. 1984, 3.

5. Neal A. Maxwell, *The Promise of Discipleship*, Deseret Book, Salt Lake City, Utah, 2001, 111. (Recently released in soft cover.)

6. Tad R. Callister, *The Infinite Atonement,* Deseret Book, Salt Lake City, Utah, 2000, 79.

7. Dunn and Eyre, *The Birth That We Call Death,* Bookcraft, 1976, 27—quoting from *Journal of Discourses.*

8. Lorenzo Snow, "Preaching the Gospel in the Spirit World," *Collected Discourses,* 363.

9. Robert L. Millet, *When a Child Wanders,* Deseret Book, 2005, 127.

10. in Conference Report, Apr. 1929, 110; emphasis added.

11. Neal A. Maxwell, *The Promise of Discipleship,* 2001, 111.

12. Dale C. Mouritsen, "The Spirit World, Our Next Home," *Ensign,* Jan. 1977, 47.

3

Glimpses beyond the Veil

I will go before your face.
I will be on your right hand and on your left,
and my Spirit shall be in your hearts,
and mine angels round about you, to bear you up.

D&C 84:88

I have been greatly uplifted by the words of others who have lost loved ones to suicide. A mother, who had also lost a son, e-mailed me:

I discovered as you have, that through the pain of it all, the Lord does walk with us. He will continue to help you each step of the way. There are rich spiritual experiences that come from having a child on the other side of the veil. The veil becomes very thin. To this I can bear strong witness. There are things you learn from experiences like these that we can learn no other way.

Brenda Floyd often dreams of her son and said:

In every dream the very first words I say to him are, "I love you!" Not that we never clashed, but Danny's heart was very tender and compassionate toward me all his life. It still is. When he is near, I feel enveloped. I can tell he is here. Oh how I wish I could part the veil and just take a peek.

Brenda's wish is one most of us have made and that some have had come true. I have mixed feelings about sharing specific experiences that others have had with departed loved ones. There is always the danger of setting up expectations that may not be met. Spiritual manifestations cannot be demanded or forced. Several mothers e-mailed me after I wrote an article in *Meridian Magazine* (online) about Brian's death, telling me they had sensed their child's presence and had been reassured. I couldn't help but wonder why I hadn't been blessed with the same experiences. It has taken time for me to be content with my own different assurances.

We don't know why some people receive personal visits from a loved one after they have departed and others don't. Sometimes our greatest trial of faith may be when we do *not* receive the specific spiritual manifestation we desire. But we are instructed not to seek for signs, but for understanding. Only the Lord knows what experience each individual is prepared for, will accept, or will be nurtured by. It is also important to remember that pain, guilt, anxiety, depression, and noise can mask not only whisperings of the spirit, but also communication of love from the spirit world.

Dee Oviatt said, "I recently had a couple of thoughts while praying that I felt were inspiration. One was, 'You are so full of sorrow that I cannot reach you.' The second was that I must reach a point where the joy of knowing Laura and having her as one of my children outweighs the pain and tragedy of her death."

Another theory is that the ability to discern the presence of spirits is one of the Gifts of the Spirit, and none of us are given all the gifts. Remember in 1 Corinthians 12 when Paul talks about spiritual gifts? Just as the body has need of all its parts, and the eyes can't do the job of the ears, he infers that all of us are given different spiritual gifts—that we may have need of each other and help each other. I have not been granted this particular gift and sometimes have yearned for it. Those who have it need to use caution in sharing.

To illustrate, here's a true story that was e-mailed to me: Two women, we'll call Beth and Jill, who had both lost sons to suicide, met in a store. Jill told Beth that her son had appeared to her and assured her that he was fine. She glibly said she knew *Beth's* son was fine too. Beth was repelled by the very words that Jill meant to be comforting. She felt Jill had no way of knowing that someone else's son was fine just because her own was.

Beth's heart hurt that the woman had received such a reassurance and she herself had been left to wonder—and she questioned her sharing it with someone she barely knew in such a public setting. Spiritual experiences should be treated with great respect. And we need to remember that such experiences should be treasured and shared only as the Spirit prompts.

Still, the experiences of others, when shared appropriately, can offer comfort and act as building blocks for our faith. I marvel to know that the veil is so thin. So I'm going to risk more sharing. I encourage you, my dear readers, to pray and ask for the Spirit to confirm truth as it pertains to you.

Our Loved Ones Can Be Assigned to Help Us

Several mothers have told me they have felt the presence of their departed child and have been assured that they are working in a mighty way for the welfare of their family on the earth.

A mother named Sherry e-mailed me several years ago with this message:

> As a mother who has just gone through the fourth anniversary of a son's untimely death . . . I can tell you many things . . . I know for a fact that he is doing oh so much more than one could imagine for [his] family on this side of the veil. I cannot tell you the blessings which come to our family through his hands working on the other side . . . As it is written in the booklet you quoted, the ones who pass on do work and work hard, but after they gain their knowledge and have started the repentance process they [may even be] allowed to visit. I know that Heavenly Father and Mother both have special places in their hearts for those [of us] who are left. They understand the coulda, shoulda,

woulda syndrome, as I call it. The Veil is thin, I testify of this. Oh the sweet gospel peace, the knowledge that they are there with us, beside us and watching over us. Knowing that when my house is quiet, and being home alone and just listening, I can feel his spirit give me a hug.

I was fascinated and heartened by Lance Richardson's book, *The Message*, where he tells about his near-death experience, visiting the spirit world when his body was in a coma. A grandfather, cousin, and uncle (who had died previously) had messages for Lance, in which he learned, and even witnessed the reality of angel ministrations. Lance (as a spirit) accompanied his grandfather's spirit to deliver a message to a family member here. Then, his cousin, Randy, who had died twenty years before, said: "Lance, do you understand what I am saying to you? I have helped you many times in your life. I have been given assignments on several occasions to assist you and inspire you." His Uncle Howard added, "I, too, have similar assignments," he explained. "There is other work I must do, as well, but I am often called upon to help my wife and children who are yet in mortality."

Lance concluded: "I had never understood nor thought of how God delivers assistance to us. With billions of children, what more perfect plan could he use than through righteous family members? It made me think about how often I may have been given inspiration from God through ministering 'family' servants of God . . . I felt that burning warmth inside, testifying to me that it was true."[1]

One thing I know for sure—when you have someone you deeply love in the spirit world, the connection with that realm is stronger, more real. That connection can be a spiritual strength and a safeguard against the power of the destroyer.

Personal Assurance

While I have not had a sure sense of Brian's presence, I have received assurances from others who have. My son's former girlfriend, still single, contacted me after his death. She had a sincere love for him, grieved his death, and was concerned for my welfare. Once, when I was having an especially difficult time, she e-mailed me:

> *Hi Darla, I just had a sort of strange experience that Brian was present. I started to pray and Brian kissed me on the forehead and said something like, "make sure my mother is okay" or "take care of my mother," or something to that effect. It was quite strange, but it was a good feeling. Anyway, I had the strong feeling that perhaps you may be having a hard time and needed to hear that Brian is watching over you. I love you, Stacey.*

Can you imagine the tears and sweet feelings that e-mail brought? I received even greater assurance from my dear friend and teacher from my high school days, Vera Infelt. She was not a member of the Church, but a deeply spiritual woman. She was ninety-seven when, about two months after Brian's death, she had a visit from him. (She told me that nothing like this had ever happened to her before.) She had been sitting alone in the courtyard of the assisted living center, bundled up against the November cold, enjoying the fresh air and the stars, but thinking deeply about me and my sorrow. Suddenly Brian was there. She told me three times about this experience and each time I wrote down what she said.

Brian said, "You love my mother; that's why you feel my presence now." She asked him, "Why did you do what you did? It upset your mother terribly." He didn't answer the question, but smiled and said, "I'm happier now. I'm in reality. I want people who cared about me to know that I'm all right. I want you to tell them I'm okay. I wasn't a perfect person, but I expect to be. People will think I was a coward, but I'm not."

Vera said, "Your mother misses you so much." Brian replied, "I feel like I'm with her. I've never really been separated from her—NOT EVER! We always shared something. We'll always have each other, and I'll be with her again." (This was a surprise and a consolation to me, especially in light of the five years Brian spent totally away from me and the family.)

She couldn't remember what else they talked about, but she felt like Brian's life there is now full of smiles. Just before he left, Brian gave her a little kiss on the forehead; and then he was gone. She was left with the sense that everything was all right, and the heavy feelings she had been having about him lifted. Vera said, "I know it took him awhile, but he's doing well. I have such a feeling of acceptance of it all now."

I asked Vera to give Brian messages from me because I knew she didn't have long to live. She entered the spirit world not many months later. I am comforted every time I think about Vera, whose love and caring brought her such a sweet experience with my son.

The only time I, myself, have had any sense of Brian's actual presence is in dreams—and I simply don't know whether a vivid dream of a departed person means they were visiting. But one dream stands out:

> *I entered a large hall where dozens of my family members were sitting down together at long tables. Some I was seeing had already died. Others are still alive. As I walked farther into the room, I saw Brian at the head of one of the tables. I ran over to him, full of joy, and said, "Oh Brian, you're here!" He stood and embraced me and said simply, "Of course I'm here, Mom."*

I woke up feeling wonderful. That was all there was to it, but the symbolism seems important.

Trusting God's Infinite Care

The comfort keeps coming; the answers become clearer. I spoke with a friend a few weeks after Brian died. I had known her only as a fine writer, a woman of great insight. I learned that her mother and her brother had both died by suicide. She spoke matter-of-factly, with words something like this: "Of course your son is being given every possible opportunity to learn and progress. Of course he is being loved and healed. Why wouldn't he be, considering all we know about God's love and mercy?"

And I thought, of course. It is so simple, so sure. I believe it all; oh Lord, help thou my unbelief in moments when I doubt and fall into fear for Brian.

I must trust God with my son. Why should that be hard? In Matthew 7:9-11 we read, "Or what man is there of you, whom if his son ask bread, will he give him a stone? Or if he ask a fish, will he give him a serpent? If ye then, being evil, know how to give good gifts unto your children, how much more shall your Father which is in heaven give good things to them that ask him?"

God's love for Brian is infinitely superior to mine. His tenderness and thoughtful care far exceed my own. Brian is okay.

I pray you will use this same line of reasoning in regard to your own loved ones who have departed this life. God will never cease loving them; they are His children. In Isaiah 49:15 we read, "Can a woman forget her sucking child, that she should not have compassion on the son of her womb? yea, they may forget, yet will I not forget thee." God's promises are sure!

Notes

1. *The Message*, American Family Publications, Idaho Falls, Idaho, 2000, 87.

Understanding and Forgiving the One Who Died

*Let us therefore come boldly
unto the throne of grace,
that we may obtain mercy,
and find grace to help
in time of need.*

Hebrews 4:16

4

Facts That Can Open Our Hearts to Understanding

And ye shall know the truth,
and the truth shall make you free.

John 8:32

One father, who had recently lost his daughter to suicide said:

My initial reaction has been to say nothing but nice things
about my daughter and dwell on the good memories. But I
know that my anger with her is just over the horizon. And I'm going to
need to deal with being very angry at her for what she has done to me
and the rest of our family.

So many caring individuals who have been impacted by suicide are left to clean up the mess of their own broken hearts and confused feelings. Families must also deal with the financial burden, personal belongings that must be disposed of, and sometimes children left behind. The impact on children or siblings can be devastating.

Sooner or later we have to deal with our anger at the person who died for the anguish and serious problems they have caused us and others. Admitting our feelings is important! Anger and emotional turmoil can *decrease* as understanding increases. Educating ourselves concerning the probable brain dysfunction of those who could no longer deal with their emotional pain is essential to our healing.

When someone you love dies from a disease or an accident, you remember him in relation to his life, not his death. But in the case of suicide we are all too likely to focus on the death. We may go over and over the details, trying to answer the "whys," instead of moving ahead.

To any person with a normally functioning brain, suicide is totally inexplicable. We can't imagine how they could have done it and we may judge them harshly. We may never know how many valiant battles our loved one may have fought and won before losing this one particular battle. And it seems unfair that all the good acts should be forgotten or blotted out by his or her final act.

Dee Oviatt's daughter, Laura, knew, loved, and lived the gospel—but her faithfulness did not spare her years of torment from mental illness and depression that no treatment seemed to help. A friend sent Dee a message, sharing an analogy concerning his daughter's suicide. Dee said:

> *My friend compared Laura's taking of her life to someone jumping from a burning building and told me we could no more blame Laura for what she did than we could blame someone for choosing to jump in order to escape being burned to death.*
>
> *I weep when I think about Laura being in a position where she honestly and truly felt, as she indicated in the note she left behind, that she had no other alternative than to take her life. My heart breaks at the thoughts of what this must have been like for her and how I could do nothing to help her. (Laura also said in her note that she didn't believe me when I told her that things would get better.)*

Still, it's natural to blame those that complete a suicide for the grief they've caused us. But the blame needs to be on the illness or other mitigating factors, not on the person seeking refuge the only way they knew how.

So Many Contributing Factors

For more than a decade Mary Pleshette Willis had been in denial about her father's suicide and had buried her feelings about it. Then she participated in a program at the University of Pittsburgh Medical Center called Survivors of Suicide (SOS).

In this SOS course, Mary learned that it is often the improper functioning of the brain, not the situation, that people who complete suicide have in common. Millions suffer from depression and addictions and don't take their own lives. However, a combination of factors—physiological, psychological, environmental, and genetic—can sometimes converge at a critical moment to push someone over the edge. The article called it a kind of a "brain attack."

Mary said that after she received that understanding she was able to let go of her anger, quit blaming her dad for the way he died, and quit blaming herself for anything she might have done or not done. She learned that how much you can let go of determines how much you can grow.[1]

The basic premise of the article is that chemical imbalance and malfunction of the brain play a big part in most suicides. Some say that suicide victims die of an illness just as surely as if they had died of cancer. Every situation is different because of the myriad factors involved.

Looking at the Contributing Factors

Debbie Bake, who has experienced suicidal depression (and later became a Behavioral Health Specialist working with suicidal people and their families), has made a major contribution to this book. Check out the Resource section at the back of this book for her thoughts on cognitive behavioral therapy, as well as the mindset of those who attempt suicide. Her clear and powerful words are sure to add to your level of understanding.

She helped me understand the complexity of the issues we face when we are trying to comprehend how our loved one could do what they did.

Studying Debbie's graphic on the next page (43) helps me recognize patterns and contributing factors. Brian had issues in every area listed in the chart.

This clear representation of the many factors contributing to major depression is of particular interest to those of us who have lost a loved one to suicide because we could also call the graph, "contributing factors which may lead to suicide." The graph is also applicable because major depression is the one thing suicide victims are most likely to have in common. Each circle is intertwined, signifying the inseparable connection between the biological, environmental, psychological and spiritual areas in one's life.

Education concerning the contributing factors is helpful because we humans are so inclined to make wrong assumptions when we don't know the facts. We are grasping for explanations and for someone or something to blame. None of us know the thinking ability, coping skills, level of spirituality, situations, or body and brain disorders of anyone else. That is why judging those who die by suicide must be left to God. He is the only one who sees the whole picture, including the intentions of the each person's heart.

Counselor, Russ Siegenberg said:

> *Research shows that heredity is a clear factor in depression, so we might conclude that some people have tendencies toward depression. However, other factors such as abuse, trauma, life environment, drug use, physical illness, level of resiliency, religion, and coping skills play significant roles as well. There is some evidence that depressed people have hypofrontality (less energy in the frontal lobe) so that they are less able to think clearly and reason while in a depression, and thus less accountable.*
>
> *I do think it is reasonable to say that if there were a single, clear biological cause, then medications would help more than they do. Medicine is moderately effective for 1/2 to 2/3 of depressed people, but much less so for the chronically depressed or those with bipolar disorder. False beliefs*

Factors That Contribute to Major Depression

Environmental Factors

Loss of job
Financial difficulties
Problematic relationships
Dismantled support system
Unmet needs
Lack of acceptance by peers
Abuse/Chaos/Violence

Biological Factors

Heredity
Hormonal irregularities
   (male & female)
Neurotransmitter levels
Chronic pain
Inadequate Vitamin D
Medical conditions
   ➤ Addictions
   ➤ Diabetes
   ➤ Eating disorders
      (especially
      anorexia)
   ➤ Thyroid disease
   ➤ Sleep disorders
Medications
   ➤ Prednisone
   ➤ Narcotic pain meds
   ➤ Beta blockers

Psychological Factors

Chronic worry
   ➤ Fear
   ➤ Anxiety
Unresolved emotions
   ➤ Grief/Loss/Trauma
Thinking errors
   ➤ All or nothing
   ➤ Chronic pessimism
   ➤ Excessive and
      inappropriate guilt
   ➤ Self-criticism
   ➤ Perfectionism
Poor coping skills
   ➤ Unmanaged stress
   ➤ Ineffective problem-
      solving techniques
Hopelessness
   ➤ Suicidal ideation

Environment

Biology

Psych.

Spiritual

Spiritual Factors

Spiritual deprivation
Lifestyle incongruent with beliefs
Failure to appreciate ramifications of being a literal child of God
Extending mercy to others but not to one's self
Poor understanding of the healing power of the Atonement
Underdevelopment of potential
Bitterness toward God when bad things happen to good people
Estranged from nature and beauty

Created by
Debbie Bake
© 2011

are also a major culprit (and they, of course, come from the father of lies). I have no doubt that believing false ideas further compromises the sensitive biology of depression-prone individuals. There is no lasting depression without hopelessness. The whole subject is a very complex one.

Focusing In

While we are making major strides in our society, most of us are still woefully lacking in understanding, especially of mental illness (including major depression) and of addiction—which can also be a major contributing factor to the probability of suicide. Consequently, I'm including a summary of information that has helped me understand these two factors.

1. Mental Illness

I can safely say it is a rare exception for someone in his right mind to make the choice to kill himself. Our society downplays depression as a causative factor for suicide, often choosing to blame a disappointment or failure in life. But everyone experiences hard times; it isn't the situation, but people's unhealthy responses and dysfunctional brains that push them over the edge. If hard times caused suicide, how many adults would be left alive?

Though statistics vary, most sources credit as high as ninety percent of suicides to severe depression—a form of mental illness that can make life a living nightmare. Yet, the majority of depressed people don't attribute their feelings of failure to the disease; they believe it comes from their own flawed characters. Many deny they are even depressed, believing their negative and distorted thinking is reality. Most feel worthless, and don't realize the feeling is not a fact.

I have recently seen a vivid example. A friend's sister who died by suicide as I was finishing this book had adamantly claimed she wasn't depressed or suicidal—when both tendencies were clearly evident. Her relatives feared for her life for months, especially when she made out a will and began to disperse her funds. But she absolutely denied she was suicidal and refused to get help.

There are many reasons people refuse help. Seeking psychiatric help is still sorely stigmatized. Your loved one may have seen others whose careers were destroyed by the label of mental illness. Some people may lack the necessary referral they need to see a specialist. Others may not understand what is involved in therapy, or might be unwilling to undergo the process. And of course, many find themselves lacking the necessary funds required to receive needed treatment.

The past president of the Alberta Mental Health Association recently offered another part of the explanation. She said *that most people who commit suicide believe there is nothing that can help them, so why waste time, energy, money, just to get told they can't be helped, and risk MORE helplessness and hopelessness and rejection.* Especially if they have already experienced many ineffective treatments, they believe they are basically flawed in character and not "fixable."

In reality, it is not "want of character" that threatens them but the palpable disease of depression: as real as diabetes, and ten times more deadly. To complicate things, desperation for relief from the darkness of severe depression and other mental illnesses often propels people into substance abuse, which makes the picture even darker. Any combination of mental illness and substance abuse can totally rob people of a normal ability to cope with adverse circumstances or make good choices. When suicidal thoughts enter in, such individuals have no capacity to think rationally in order to combat their suicidal thoughts because the brain is simply malfunctioning. That describes what I know of my son's situation.

Since normal brains trigger a survival instinct that keeps people alive in the midst of the most extreme trials, we have to remember that a person who completes suicide may have been impacted by an illness as real as any other illness. The sad thing is that—even in death—people suffering from mental illness are *not* often granted the respect and empathy given those suffering from other diseases. In the same way, suicide grievers are not given the same kind of empathy as those who have lost a loved one to a more "respectable" disease.

In the *Salt Lake Tribune*, June 24, 2009, Michael A. Kalm (past president of the Utah Psychiatric Association), wrote a piece called "Struggle with

Mental Illness Is Also Valiant." It is vivid and illuminating. When I read it, I thought of my son. Here are some excerpts:

> *Two quotes from today's Tribune: In the Obituaries section, "died . . . after a valiant struggle with breast cancer." And in an article on Meriwether Lewis in the Faith section, "The idea of besmirching his memory by saying he committed suicide is not a very positive image of his personality and accomplishments."*
>
> *What's wrong with this picture? Plenty. How is it that someone dying after struggling with the dread disease of cancer is seen as "valiant," while someone dying after struggling with the dread disease of depression is seen as having a "besmirched memory"?*
>
> *It is ironic that these two quotes appeared at this time. I had just finished writing an article for the Utah Psychiatric Association . . . that includes a fantasized conversation with Thomas Jefferson and Meriwether Lewis [who suffered with mental illness that later led to an apparent suicide]. Jefferson was sending Lewis to lead the Corps of Discovery on its epic journey through the Louisiana Territory. Jefferson was not only Lewis's mentor, he acted very much as Lewis's surrogate father.*
>
> *Jefferson seemed to have a keen insight into the demons that Lewis struggled with, and in an age before psychiatric treatments, knew just how to nurture and support him, help him realize his talents and not become victim to his terrible adversity. Lewis, in turn, was fiercely loyal to Jefferson, risking his life again and again to do research that would please his mentor.*
>
> *Jefferson knew of Lewis's demons, but never equated them with who Lewis was as a person. He described Lewis, "Of courage undaunted, possessing a firmness and perseverance of purpose which nothing but impossibilities could divert from its direction . . . honest . . . of sound understanding and a fidelity to truth so scrupulous that whatever he should report would be as certain as if seen by ourselves . . . I could have no hesitation in confiding the enterprise to him." . . .*

It is time for us now, in the 21ˢᵗ century, to know what Jefferson knew 200 years ago: A disease, a mental illness, does not define who a person is. A person is ultimately his hopes, his aspirations, his courage, and his actions. These should never be confused with his disease.

Lewis's memory, far from besmirched, is shining bright, as is the memory of all who struggle valiantly against disease, physical and mental.

Hyrum Smith, speaking at a funeral for a friend who died by suicide, said:

Does the mistake Lowell made the other night blot out all of the good that this man did in his life? No! . . . Lowell was a wonderful missionary. He was a great father. He was a great man. He was dedicated to his Father in Heaven. Like many of us, he made some mistakes, one big one. It doesn't blot out everything he was.[2]

When someone we love dies by way of suicide, neither the good things about them nor our capacity to love is lost. Remembering the love we have for them is good. Even praying for them in their new situation is good. Remembering can be healing, especially if we focus on the whole person, not just the problem areas.

Many who suffer from mental illness do not have the benefit of family or friends who demonstrate the kind of love and respect that Jefferson showed for Lewis. Even when there is support, self-worth inevitably takes a hit.

Mental Health worker, Debbie Bake, tells about working with patients on the psychiatric unit in the hospital. Many patients were there because of suicide attempts. She said:

It soon became my mission to help patients understand their true worth, but I wondered how I could do that in a hospital setting. After asking the Lord for His guidance it occurred to me that those with depression believe that they are their illness with its corresponding symptoms. I pondered what a depressed patient would be without their illness identity, and it gave me an idea. When I taught group one day, we discussed what was impacting their self-esteem.

I asked each person to take a piece of paper and write as quickly as they could one-word character traits they ascribed to themselves (either now or in the past, positive and negative alike). I urged them to hurry so they wouldn't get stuck thinking only of the negative, dominate traits. Then I asked them to cross out those traits that were linked in any way to their illness. I explained that whatever was left not crossed out was a more accurate depiction of who they really are. I was thrilled to see so many faces that had previously had no expression light up. Afterwards, several patients told me it was the first time they ever thought of themselves as separate from their illness, that perhaps there was a possibility their true selves still existed.

The most important thing to remember is this: a person is not his illness. The spirit identity over-rides all other factors and will continue even after death.

The best LDS book I have read on mental illness is *Valley of Sorrow: A Layman's Guide to Understanding Mental Illness* by Alexander B. Morrison, an emeritus General Authority. Elder Morrison's daughter has suffered all her life with a mental illness that no treatment has been able to alleviate—which had led him to in-depth study and understanding of the subject. His gospel perspectives are invaluable, and I hope you will take the time to read his book.

2. The Addiction Factor

A wide range of addictions often factor into the downward slide toward suicide. A good resource for understanding the addiction factor that many of our loved ones struggled with is *Understanding Alcohol and Drug Addiction: An LDS Perspective.*[3]

Addiction is simply one of the most difficult problems a person can grapple with. Often our loved ones may have struggled with multiple addictions and were so discouraged with their inability to overcome that they felt, "why keep trying?"

I know in Brian's case, his addictions chipped away at his feelings of worth. He quit smoking over and over—but in moments of extreme stress he kept going back to it. His feeling of failure must have increased each time he returned to a behavior he knew was hurting him. I'm sure it was the same with his Marijuana addiction. In my reading about this particular drug, one article suggested that the initial feelings one gets from this drug might be considered the devil's counterfeit for the spiritual peace of sitting in the celestial room in the temple. For sensitive people who so much desire peace and don't know where to find it, the lure of that momentary feeling, coupled with the physical craving that comes with addiction, can be overpowering. Addiction is such a powerful force that those of us who have not been held captive by it cannot even imagine how difficult it is.

No wonder the adversary works so diligently to draw those who are discouraged or mentally ill into addictions. Any addiction increases the degree of difficulty and decreases the person's ability to hear the promptings of the Spirit. Addiction takes over a person's will and can rob one of the power to decide.

Elder Boyd K. Packer's explanation in his article "Revelation in a Changing World," is the best I've read. He said that narcotic addiction serves the design of the prince of darkness because it disrupts the channel to the holy spirit of truth.[4]

Spiritual Starvation

I honestly feel that one of the contributing factors to Brian's death was spiritual starvation. We live in a world that is drastically short on spiritual edification. Very few movies or TV shows feed the soul. The fast pace and complicated demands of our society tend to drain rather than nurture. Technology has taken us one step further from our natural connection with nature. It takes a concerted effort to find valid spiritual food.

Brian made very sad decisions that removed him from the spiritually edifying influence of the gospel. Most damaging, he removed himself from the influence of the Holy Ghost. On the "omission" side, he withdrew from church meetings, scriptures, and prayer. On the "commission" side he chose to break every Word of Wisdom guideline as well as the moral law. As Elder Packer points out, substance abuse and addiction literally "disrupts the channel," making it harder and harder to hear the Spirit.

Yet Brian had a very keen spiritual sense and was constantly looking for answers and trying to figure out his life. He was yearning for more understanding and went to self-help workshops and read voraciously—but nothing that drew him back to Christ.

The spirit needs daily nourishment every bit as much as the body. When a spirit doesn't get the spiritual food it needs, it becomes spiritually emaciated, weak, starved, just as the body would without food. In that condition one is much more vulnerable to the influence of the adversary. Depression is another factor that makes it difficult or impossible to feel the Spirit and inclines those so affected to search for comfort elsewhere. Factor into the equation a dysfunctional brain, and we can only begin to imagine the degree of difficulty under which many of our loved ones may have labored.

Factoring in Degree of Difficulty

Many find it easier to forgive their loved one for leaving this life once they begin to understand the extreme difficulty of living with a brain that does not function normally and disrupts their ability to feel and to think clearly. Addiction multiplies the difficulties because it affects the brain and decreases the ability to make rational and wise choices. We can be reassured that the Lord factors in the level of difficulty in His judgments (much more accurately than judges of athletic events are able to do), and so should we. Education can greatly increase our empathy for the level of difficulty our loved ones labored under.

Notes

1. See "My Father's Sweater," *Reader's Digest,* Dec. 2005, pp. 61-62, 64-65.

2. Hyrum W. Smith, *My Peace I Give Unto You,* Covenant Communications, American Fork, Utah, 2004. (Both audio and booklet out of print, but used copies may be available.)

3. Merlin O. Baker, *Understanding Alcohol and Drug Addiction: An LDS Perspective,* Cedar Fort Publishing, Springville, Utah, 2004.

4. Boyd K. Packer, "Revelation in a Changing World," *Ensign,* Nov. 1989, 14.

5

Keeping Our Focus on the Atonement

But behold, the Lord hath redeemed
my soul from hell;
I have beheld his glory,
and I am encircled about eternally
in the arms of his love.

2 Nephi 1:15

My friend Mary suggested that one of the things we learn from such extreme adversity is that "the Savior is exactly that, a savior of your sanity, a savior of your faith." He is saving me, and I know He will save each person who comes to Him with faith that He lives, faith that He loves us.

What we focus our minds on is so important because it creates our present reality. Why not focus on the Lord? In the Book of Mormon, Alma notes that when he remembered his father's teachings of Jesus and cried out to Him for mercy, a remarkable thing happened: "And now, behold, when I thought this, I could remember my pains no more; yea, I was harrowed up by the memory of my sins no more" (Alma 36:19).

Oh, is it possible? Can the Atonement actually take away the pain, even of this? Can we, too, get to the point where we remember our pains no more? Yes. The scriptural promises are sure. But it is easy to forget the peace that comes from Jesus when waves of grief wash over us. For this reason, I cherish this verse: "Take heed to thyself, and keep thy soul diligently, lest thou forget the things which thine eyes have seen, and lest they depart from thy heart all the days of thy life" (Deuteronomy 4:9).

I, like most life-long members of the Church, have had numerous witnesses of the Spirit in regard to the Savior and His mission. I need to remind myself of all the times the Holy Ghost has borne witness to my heart that Jesus is the Christ and that His Atonement is real. His atoning blood covers the pain and heartache that our loved ones' sins have caused us. It covers what we do and what is done to us—whether others choose to repent or not—because the Atonement covers ALL pain. "He [the Savior] shall go forth, suffering pains and afflictions and temptations of every kind; and this that the word might be fulfilled which saith he will take upon him the pains and the sicknesses of his people" (Alma 7:11).

We can choose to carry the hurt or we can let the Savior, through His Atonement, carry the load. We have agency and can choose to stay burdened down with the pain of the suicide or we can choose to accept what the Savior has already done for us—which will help our loved one as well as us. Surely their greatest desire is for us to turn to Christ and feel the perfect brightness of hope that He offers.

If we accept His Atonement, we don't need to suffer indefinitely. We heal so much more quickly when we let Him take our pain. Sometimes I've said, "But how?" And the answer seems to come: "Just believe that He will take it and He will." Not all at once, but He takes the part we cannot bear. Some of the pain is necessary for the lessons we still must learn.

"That Our Children May Know . . ."

I'm so sorry I did not recognize how central the message of the Atonement is in the gospel until Brian was out of our home. Oh, how I wish I'd known and understood so I could have somehow reached him with that good news, because when he was an adult he didn't want to hear it. In Brian's most impressionable years I thought my job was to do all the right things and teach my children to do all the right things. Now I know that a parent's job is to teach where to go for a remission of sins: "And we talk of Christ, we rejoice in Christ, we preach of Christ, we prophesy of Christ, and we write according to our prophecies, that our children may know to what source they may look for a remission of their sins" (2 Nephi 25:26; emphasis added).

A sign in Brian's own handwriting hung on the wall of his apartment that said: "Life is not an exact science. Life is an art. Life is the art of drawing sufficient conclusions from insufficient premises." The only sufficient premises are found in the doctrines of Christ and the need we all have to depend daily on His love, grace and mercy. In this life Brian didn't know that Jesus makes up the difference after all we can do. I know that Brian is now in a situation where he is truly learning the power of the Atonement and is able to experience the love of Christ.

The Lord Alone Can Judge

At Brian's funeral, my son Scott read a quote by Brigham Young that continues to be thought-provoking to me. He said that President Young talked about when the books are opened, out of which the human family are to be judged, how disappointed the hypocrites and Pharisees will be to see many enter the kingdom of heaven before them that they judged least likely—because the Lord knew they never designed to do wrong; that the devil had power over them, and they suffered in their mortal state a thousand times more than the "miserable hypocritical Pharisees."[1] We know so little of the suffering of others and are simply not to judge.

"Father, Forgive Them; for They Know Not What They Do"

Brian's suicide brought grief to many. However, my conclusion in regard to forgiving Brian is that there is really nothing for me to forgive. His sins, which are not for me to judge, are between Brian and his Maker, and the Atonement is more than adequate to pay for them. He did the best he could with what he had to work with. He struggled valiantly; he tried his best to be true to his perceptions of truth. What more could the Lord ask of any of us?

At Brian's memorial service, our bishop was the concluding speaker. He said that in the days he had been pondering this situation only one scripture had come repeatedly to his mind: the Savior's words from the cross as He looked down with compassion on those who were putting Him to death: "Father, forgive them; for they know not what they do" (Luke 23:34). He said he felt strongly that Jesus was at this moment interceding for Brian with the Father and saying, "Father, forgive Brian, for he knew not what he was doing." He said that the Lord is infinitely merciful and forgiving and that He would give Brian the most grace and love and mercy that He possibly could.

I believe these same comforting words apply to most, if not all suicide cases. "Father, forgive them" is what the Atonement is all about. Jesus did His part and made forgiveness possible. And surely sins of ignorance are the easiest for Him to forgive.

I have sought forgiveness for every feeling of anger I have ever harbored towards Brian for his suicide decision. Surely suicide is a sin committed in ignorance. Even if he thought he knew, Brian didn't *really* know what he was doing. And he didn't have the slightest realization of the grief his act would bring so many. Father, forgive him; for he knew not what he did. Father, forgive me; for I knew not what I did whenever I hurt Brian or felt there was much in him I needed to forgive. Father, forgive every one of us for all the times we simply don't know what we are doing.

Notes

1. See Brigham Young, "How and By Whom Zion Is to Be Built," *Journal of Discourses*, vol. 10, 176.

Learning to Forgive Others

*Shouldest not thou also have had
compassion on thy fellowservant,
even as I had pity on thee?*

Matthew 18:33

6

Anger, Hurt, and Blame

Let us therefore come boldly unto the throne of grace,
that we may obtain mercy,
and find grace to help in time of need.

Hebrews 4:16

*T*rauma of the magnitude of a suicide in the family brings up old issues and hurts. It made me acutely aware of improvements I needed to make in my relationship with myself and with others; a spotlight was shone on what I needed to change. Another natural reaction to tragedy is to try to find reasons for what has happened. And that may lead to casting blame.

When a relationship (such as marriage) is already in disrepair it is easy to blame each other in a time of tragedy. Divorce rates skyrocket in the aftermath. Had I *not* already been divorced from Brian's father, this event could have been the straw that broke the camel's back. Divorced or not, the issue of blame is a big one that must be dealt with. While casting blame is a predictable result of the brain's need to make sense of something as inexplicable as suicide, it is always counter-productive.

We can choose to change and grow and forgive in this situation or we can choose to blame, put up walls, and draw far apart. The most dangerous choice is to blame God, or even draw ourselves far apart from God by courting angry feelings.

The Surprise Emotion: Anger

I expected to deal with grief after Brian's death, but not anger. Yet that is what I was feeling soon after the dust settled. I knew many contributing factors, such as Brian's terrible depression (part of his bipolar disorder), coupled with his own poor choices, had brought him to his crisis; still I felt angry at everything and everybody that could have contributed to his problems. I was angry at myself, my former spouse, and my other children for not being able to give Brian more of what he needed. Angry that despite all my righteous desires I was still so lacking in regard to relationships in general.

I was angry at Brian's school friends, church friends, anyone who used to tease him. I was angry at the person who recently stole Brian's prized electric guitar. I was angry at business associates who took advantage of him and weren't fair to him, friends who didn't honor their agreements. I was angry at Brian for closing his mind to the possibility that the biggest thing he was missing in his life was the gospel, and for not telling anyone how bad he was feeling. I was even angry at the Lord for placing Brian in this particular set of circumstances and for knowing what was going to happen and not somehow prompting even one of us who loved Brian to go rescue him, stop him!

Now, added to that, I felt reason to resent others for hurtful responses (or lack of responses) to our tragedy. No one in my immediate circle at church had ever been through anything like this. They didn't know what to say, so it was easier to avoid me. I was treated differently; I felt I had lost the respect I formerly enjoyed. While no one said anything overtly unkind, I felt ignored and misunderstood. And there was no appropriate setting to explain anything.

The jaws of temptation were open wide to dwell on the slights, the hurts (and hurt is often expressed as anger). When my anger extended to the Lord

I questioned why He didn't put Brian in a different home or bring different people into his life to help him. I just kept thinking that the Lord could have made all this turn out differently! And I kept feeling the need to cast blame. Because of all I'd read, I knew the only way to sidestep these temptations was to learn to truly forgive, but I wasn't sure how to do that.

The Lord Merely Asks Us to Be Willing

A couple of months after Brian's death I went and talked to my kind bishop, Jeffrey Edwards. His counsel felt so inspired, so simple, so right. He said to look forward—not back. He counseled me to recognize that the feelings of anger and hurt I was having were normal, and that I should not beat myself up for them; instead, I should express my willingness in prayer to let the Lord take them from me. He told me the Corrie ten Boom story—one I sorely needed to be reminded of.

Corrie and her sister Betsie were sent to Ravensbruck concentration camp for the "crime" of harboring Jews. Betsie died there. Years later Corrie told a powerful experience she had with a former captor. She had just spoken to a group of people in a church in Munich, Germany, giving the message that God forgives.

Afterwards, a man approached her; she recognized him and her heart turned cold. He told her that since the days he had been a guard in Ravensbruck he had become a Christian and knew God had forgiven him for the cruel things he did there. Then he asked something that was very difficult for Corrie. He said, "I would like to hear it from your lips as well. Fraulein; will you forgive me?" And he stretched out his hand, imploring her to take it.

Corrie reports, "And I stood there – I whose sins had every day to be forgiven – and could not. Betsie had died in that place – could he erase her slow, terrible death simply for the asking?" She reminded herself of Jesus' words, "If you do not forgive men their trespasses, neither will your Father in heaven forgive your trespasses."

But she had taught others that forgiveness is not an emotion, but a choice. She knew she must make that choice, regardless of the temperature of her heart. "Jesus, help me!" she prayed silently, "I can lift my hand. I can do that much. You supply the feeling."

Woodenly, mechanically, she thrust her hand into the guard's. As she did, an amazing thing happened. Here's how she describes it:

> *The current started in my shoulder, seemed to flood my whole being, bringing tears to my eyes. "I forgive you, brother," I cried. "With all my heart." For a long moment we grasped each others' hand, the former guard and the former prisoner. I had never known God's love so intensely as I did then.*[1]

Bishop Edwards said something like, "Tell the Lord that you, like Corrie, are *willing* to forgive and let go of the bad feelings, but acknowledge that only He has the power to complete the healing process of forgiveness. Expect that angry feelings and grief feelings will continue to surface now and then. Healing is a long-term process. Just feel the hurt, feel the anger. Then give it all to the Lord." He said to ask the Lord in any moment of pain to apply the healing blood of the Savior, then move on. He counseled me to ask the Lord to help me forgive and to feel His forgiveness *every time* bad feelings come up.

Over time I learned that when I surrender my anger, blame, or unforgiving feelings I open the door for love to flow in. Progress depends on how much of my grief and anger and pain I am willing to surrender to the Lord. Holding on to grief and pain impedes my healing.

Sometimes, after Brian's suicide, I got depressed because I *wanted* to surrender my bad feelings to the Lord but had no idea *how*. It doesn't do us any good to know *what we* should do if we don't know *how to do it!* Consequently, I'm including many how-to's in the rest of this book.

Notes

1. Corrie ten Boom, *Clippings from My Notebook*, 92.

7

We Want to Let Go of Bad Feelings, but How?

God hath not given us the spirit of fear, but of power,
and of love and of a sound mind.

2 Timothy 1:7

*I*n an excellent article, "Live in Thanksgiving Daily,"[1] Elder Joseph B. Wirthlin counseled us to let go of the negative emotions that bind our hearts. He explained the many benefits of filling our souls with love, faith, and thanksgiving, and made it clear that anger, resentment, and bitterness stunt our spiritual growth.

Who doesn't want to let go of bad feelings? But I kept stumbling over questions of exactly how to do that. The "how" begins with desire. Here's how Alma tells us to begin: "If ye will awake and arouse your faculties, even to an experiment upon my words, and exercise a particle of faith, yea even if ye can no more than desire to believe . . ." A particle isn't much. And why should we resist trying an experiment—believing just enough to try and see what happens? If we give even a small place for the promises of God in our hearts, our desire will be honored with His help.

Counselor Rod W. Jeppsen, in his book *"Lord I Believe; Help Thou Mine Unbelief,"* gives us this perspective:

> *We have to be willing to give up the hurt and pain so forgiveness can take its place. That's right—forgiveness replaces the hurt and pain. We do not have room in our hearts for both. At some point we either let forgiveness in or we choose to hold onto the hurt and pain. It really is our choice. We don't have to rush it. We don't have to work on someone's schedule, and forgiveness really does not have much to do with the person who offended us. It's between us and the Lord. Forgiving is what we can do only when we have the Lord's spirit in our lives and hearts. The Lord has commanded us to forgive others and I say with Nephi, "for I know that the Lord giveth no commandments unto the children of men, save he shall prepare a way for them that they may accomplish the thing which he commandeth them" (1 Nephi 3:7).*[2]

How does the Lord prepare the way so I can turn my bad feelings over to Him? How can I be cleansed and capable of forgiving? This is part of the repentance process. We turn to the Lord, knowing we need His help to change, to repent of our bad feelings. And we depend on our **sacramental covenants** that if we remember Him, we will have His spirit to be with us, to help us.

I've learned that a **surrender prayer** is also important. When bad feelings come up I try to remember to say: "I love Thee Father, and I am willing to let these bad feelings go, but I need Thy help. I want to give them all up to Thee. Please help me, Father; give me the strength to surrender these feelings to Thee."

Visualizations can also be helpful. I visualize my bad feelings flowing out of me like blood to a dialysis machine, asking the Lord to purify them, change them before He gives them back. At other times I visualize myself wrapping my resentments, hurts, and anger up in a soft blanket and holding them up, reaching as high as I can reach, offering them to the Lord.

My friend, Patricia, who has lost relatives to suicide, visualizes her closet as an elevator that goes clear up to heaven. She has what she calls a "God box" in her closet. When she can't deal with a particular feeling or problem, in her mind she writes about it and puts it in her God box and visualizes it going up, up, out of sight into the heavens. She asks the Lord to please deal with it for her.

Pouring our hearts out to God vocally can be cleansing. I remember one particular night when I woke up and couldn't go back to sleep. I went to the utility room—furthest away from where anyone was sleeping, closed the door, and cried out loud to the Lord. For more than an hour I poured out my laments, my sorrows, my complaints. By the time I was finished I felt relieved, even cleansed. Most importantly, I felt that the Lord listened, cared how I felt and loved me. The book *Sacred Sorrows* suggests that only the Lord can truly understand and that we should bring everything to Him.

Writing is often an effective way to give our feelings to the Lord. I can't change the past but I can change how I see it and how it affects me. Writing helps me reframe my perceptions with greater truth and understanding. Writing about a situation allows the Holy Ghost to soften my heart to those I may have bad feelings toward, and lets me glimpse the hurt they may be carrying. I often end up recognizing that my judgment of them is the thing that needs to be changed. As I write I often feel the effects of the Atonement in my own life and show my faith that the Atonement will reach and heal the lives of others as well.

Sometimes I write letters to God and pour it all out on paper, asking Him to take my negative feelings and purify and change them. If I want to make sure no one could ever read what I write, I write over each line so it is illegible, then when the page is full, tear it up and put it into the garbage. This kind of writing continues to be valuable to me for admitting and getting rid of negative feelings. I talked to a counselor who suggested burning the pages on which we pour out our bad feelings, as a symbol of being rid of them for good, as well as sending them to heaven because only the Lord can change them.

Applying: "Father, forgive them; for they know not what they do"

Pondering the whole principle of forgiveness and praying about it, I attended the temple a few months after Brian's death. My heart was full of the desire to forgive and be forgiven, but I still felt the need to understand more deeply how to accomplish it moment by moment. I silently admitted my angry feelings to the Lord and prayed for His help. I told Him how much I wanted to let go, but what a hard time I was having doing it. I knew that God's promises of forgiveness are sure, yet conditional on our forgiving one another. I was reminded of the following scripture:

> *Ye ought to forgive one another; for he that forgiveth not his brother his trespasses standeth condemned before the Lord; for there remaineth in him the greater sin.*
>
> *I, the Lord, will forgive whom I will forgive, but of you it is required to forgive all men. (D&C 64:9-10)*

I pondered about those persons I needed to forgive and asked, "How can I *fully* forgive others? Is forgiveness something you can finish or do you have to keep doing it over and over?" (I'd thought so many times that I had accomplished it—yet there I was again.) I sat for a long time in the celestial room, wrestling spiritually with this dilemma, pleading with the Lord for understanding and guidance.

Finally the same scripture came into my mind that the bishop quoted in Brian's memorial service: "Father, forgive them; for they know not what they do" (Luke 23:34).

Just thinking those words brought greater peace than I'd had for a while. The Spirit whispered convincingly that these words apply to almost any hurtful word or action in mortality and could help me let go. Do any of us—limited in perspective and knowledge, blinded by false traditions and painful past experiences—*really* know what we are doing? How much awareness is really possible of the pain we might be causing in another human heart, or the negative consequences we might be contributing to?

Isn't that an important part of what the Atonement is really about—to make up the difference for our ignorance, poor judgment, lack of understanding? In his wonderful article "The Brilliant Morning of Forgiveness," Elder Boyd K. Packer reassured us that the very purpose of the Atonement is to restore the things we cannot restore, heal the wounds we cannot heal by ourselves, and fix that which we broke and have no way of fixing.[3]

There was so much in this situation I could not restore, so much I could not fix—nor could anybody else but God.

I envisioned each person on my list, and said, "Father, forgive them; for they did not know the hurt they were causing." I felt my heart relax, and a sweet and welcome peace enter in. I turned the healing phrase to myself and said, "Father, forgive me, for I knew not what I was doing that may have hurt Brian, and I knew not how to do any better than I did." I envisioned all of us on the other side, now having the Savior's help to understand, to recognize any injury we had caused. In utter humility we asked each other's forgiveness, gratefully acknowledging the Savior's forgiveness through the Atonement, and peacefully reconciling.

Repentance is a change of mind, a fresh view about God, about oneself, and about the world. I received a fresh view that day in the temple; I received an assurance that reconciliation will some day come to pass, and that in the meantime I can trust God in all things. It was a healing process; one I enjoy repeating in my mind's eye, one I need to remind myself of.

Trust God to Help

In his book Mere Christianity, C.S. Lewis says, "After the first few steps in the Christian life we realize that everything which really needs to be done in our souls can be done only by God."[4]

I do not have the power in myself, apart from God, to overcome anger, to forgive, or access the Atonement. Only my dependence on the Lord makes it all possible. The very key to forgiving is learning to honestly express my feelings to Him, and to ask for and receive the help I need.

Forgiveness Is a Process, Not an Event

We must not fall into the trap of believing that forgiving is a one-time event—it's not something we can "finish."

Author Rod W. Jeppsen said:

> *If we look for one huge experience that will allow us to forgive, we may never find forgiveness. Forgiveness, for the most part, is made up of little changes we make over time until one day we find ourselves at peace . . . At times we may think we have forgiven and then we are hit again with resentment and anger. When we feel confused by our tendency to revisit those feelings, it's important to realize that forgiveness is an ongoing process that takes time. We must apply patience to this process and give ourselves credit for every small degree of success, knowing we'll have more later on.*[5]

I was going to need that perspective! So many situations brought up bad feelings and the need for forgiving others.

The Importance of Forgiving People for Their Reactions

To say that people in general are uncomfortable with the subject of suicide may be the understatement of the year. Consequently, even simple things become dilemmas—like how to answer when someone asks how many children you have. Do I still have five sons even if one is not on this earth? If I say, "Four living and one who passed on," the person might say, "Oh, I'm sorry. How did he die?" If I say, "suicide," I don't get sympathy, but looks of horror, averted eyes, and conversations quickly ended. I have to forgive others for reactions that, given the stigma of suicide, are to be expected.

This brings up another dilemma: When *is* it appropriate to bring up the subject of suicide? I decide who to tell about it and who not to tell by asking, "does the other person need to know?" and "do I feel prompted to share?"

Generally now, when the question comes up about number of children, I simply say I have five sons and leave it at that.

But what about the reactions of those who have known about it from the first and say unkind things? I spoke with a family who experienced not only avoidance, but openly critical and judgmental comments. Some comments are just plain insensitive. Dee Oviatt e-mailed me:

> *I had one person tell me that Laura's death was an answer to my prayers because now she is no longer suffering. I was horrified that anyone could say something so insensitive. I literally had to walk out of the room.*

People generally mean well and their intentions are good, but we must realize they cannot feel our pain and they simply don't understand. We wouldn't want them to—because the only way they *could* understand is to go through it themselves.

Still, when we are grieving we don't need to be ignored and we don't need to hear, "Aren't you over it yet?" Our hearts may be healing, but we'll never be "over it." How quickly life seems to return to normal for those minimally impacted by our tragedy, but for us, nothing will ever be the same. On the positive side, we'll never be stuck in the same ruts, the same old patterns. We'll never believe the same myths, but we'll never have the bliss of ignorance either.

In Chapter 13, starting on page 121, you will find charts of Do's and Don'ts that can help you relate to your own family and friends or anyone who is grieving a suicide. If you have a close friend who wants to know how they can help you—give them the list!

We can't control what other people say and do, but we can control how we choose to react. The following lines (an excerpt from a piece called, "Do It Anyway" by Mother Teresa, online) carry a profound message: "People are often unreasonable, illogical and self-centered: Forgive them anyway . . . You see, in the final analysis, it is between you and GOD. It was never between you and them anyway."

Hurts of the heart are an opportunity to deepen our relationship with the Lord, learn of His healing power, and partake of His miracle of forgiveness. The natural man functioning without the Spirit is totally incapable of forgiveness. The ability to forgive is a gift of the Spirit that the Savior offers to all who come unto Him.

So Much Hinges on Forgiving Others

Not forgiving others is denying the power of the Atonement to cleanse their lives. Not forgiving others limits the Lord's ability to forgive us. Not forgiving others shows we don't understand the Plan with its foundation principle of agency. When God gave us freedom of choice He knew it was a sure thing that we all would sin, so in His mercy He provided a Savior and an atonement. Not forgiving others is like saying we don't accept that atonement.

Educator Truman Madsen, in a talk on forgiveness, said: "There is no suffering beyond His ability to redeem. Refusal to forgive is refusal to accept forgiveness. Anger, bitterness, resentment, are rejections of the Atonement. Our participation in His sacrifice requires a much smaller sacrifice—giving up our enmity towards others."

To have the Lord's help and to experience what it means to forgive others is a wondrous thing. Somewhere I heard that to forgive is to set a prisoner free and discover that the prisoner was you.

Notes

1. Joseph B. Wirthlin, "Live in Thanksgiving Daily," *Ensign*, Sept. 2001, 11.

2. Rob W. Jeppsen, *Lord I Believe; Help Thou My Unbelief*, Pathway Publishing, 2005, 391.

3. See Boyd K. Packer, "The Brilliant Morning of Forgiveness," *Ensign*, Nov. 1995, 18.

4. C.S. Lewis, *Mere Christianity*, 165-66.

5. Rod W. Jeppsen, *"Lord, I Believe; Help Thou Mine Unbelief,"* Pathway Publishing, South Jordan, Utah, 2005, 360.

Mending Our Troubled Thoughts and Hearts

Be merciful unto me,
O God, be merciful unto me:
for my soul trusteth in thee:
yea, in the shadow of thy wings
will I make my refuge,
until these calamities be overpast.

Psalm 57:1

8

Suicide's Legacy of Emotional Upheaval

Deliver me out of the mire, and let me not sink . . .
Let not the waterflood overflow me,
neither let the deep swallow me up,
and let not the pit shut her mouth upon me.

Psalm 69:14-15

The aftermath of Brian's death was the Red Sea of my life: I was totally up against it and desperately in need of the Lord's rescue. A few weeks after the funeral, I was drawn to visit Brian's gravesite for the first time since his burial. It was much harder than I anticipated. The reality that his body was there, that he was gone, that I would not see him again in this life hit me all over again. I was so overcome with grief that I could not hold myself upright. First I kneeled, then collapsed on the grass by his grave and sobbed—grateful no one else was around. The day had been stormy and it began to sprinkle, and the cold rain seemed fitting. I lay there and sobbed my heart out, saying: "Oh Brian, I'm so sorry. I feel like I failed you. Please forgive me. Father in Heaven, please forgive me, and help Brian find the healing love and support there that he needs."

I finally left the cemetery but couldn't stop crying. The sorrow was so deep, so real. Yet it was better than depression because at least I felt alive. It's easy to fear and resist grief. But to open ourselves to it is to have a heart that is awake and living. Still, the weight of worry that my shortcomings and weaknesses could have contributed to Brian's despair was overwhelming. I felt I had failed.

It seems I'm not alone; the most common feeling survivors of a loved one's suicide share—especially mothers—is one of failure. A mother named April e-mailed me, telling me how her son's suicide had devastated her sense of worth. Here are some of the things she said:

> So little survived the refiner's fire of my son's death. Everything I was interested in left me. This event has changed every nook and cranny of my life and forced me to evaluate every single thing I've ever done, thought, or felt. I suddenly felt naked and vulnerable—like I was starting a new life from scratch—but this time with the knowledge of previous mistakes. I was so afraid of failing again. (I felt it was obvious that I'd failed as a mother.) So I have been trapped by this whole grief, shame, failure thing.
>
> I'm sure the Lord gets frustrated with me—so much potential down the drain. I can't seem to figure myself out since my son's death; it sort of smacked me in the face. A psychic scream of "you're not doing well!" ran through my mind. The first two years I thought I deserved to die as well since I was such a failure. I'm certain that my son had a hand in saving my life. I was so close to dying and something always happened to stop me. I just couldn't face living without him, but it was more about the fact that I couldn't forgive myself for failing him.

Feelings of failure and emotional upheaval seem to be the universal legacy of suicide. After the initial shock and numbness wore off, my mind was bombarded with questions such as, "What kind of mother has a child who kills himself? How could anyone fail more miserably than that?" Brenda Floyd said, "the only way I could describe it is that after my son's death I had no idea who I was anymore. My life was unrecognizable and I felt as though I had a mark on my forehead that said '*suicide: this mother failed her child and home.*'"

About two months after Brian's death I went alone to a stake women's conference. I looked over that big audience of good LDS women—most of them mothers—and thought, "As far as I know, I'm the only one here who has a child who has taken his own life. I can't imagine what they must think of me, but there's one thing for sure—no one here can even remotely understand how I feel." Paranoid, I began to imagine I could see judgment and accusation in people's eyes, no matter how kind they seemed to be. I talked to no one and left quickly, not staying for the luncheon afterwards.

Although the week of the funeral I'd received a great outpouring of love and support, now I felt the ward and neighborhood had withdrawn from me. Actually I was the one who had done most of the withdrawing. I felt so different, so flawed. I cried when I read the scripture, "I looked on my right hand, and behold, there was no man that would know me; refuge failed me; no man cared for my soul" (Psalm 142:4). I felt completely alone and so inferior.

It wasn't *all* in my mind, though. In defense of those of us who are experiencing a sense of isolation, it is a fact that people in general tend to avoid contact after such a tragedy. The main reason is that they don't know what to say. However, there is something else very real behind it: we are an unwelcome reminder that such things actually happen!

One of the prime purposes of this book is to help anyone who may be wading through these all-too-common feelings of failure, guilt, and isolation. I want you to know that you are *not* alone and that your worth as a person has not been decreased one iota by this horrific event—and that there is a way up and out of those feelings.

Honoring God's Plan of Agency

I grasped onto to the idea that I could not fail at someone else's stewardship. "But Brian was my stewardship," I argued. I had to learn that my influence on him was my stewardship. His choices and how he responded to my influence were not my stewardship.

We need to remember that God did not fail when one-third of His children chose against His plan and His influence. He gave those children agency and honored it. God is perfectly successful because He is perfectly true to Himself and every law and principle He teaches, not because of what His children choose to do or not do. Jesus did not fail—in spite of the fact that most of the people He taught and loved during His earthly ministry turned away.

Lehi and Sariah did not fail when Laman and Lemuel chose against what they had been taught all their lives. They succeeded because they themselves listened to the Lord's guiding voice. If Lehi and Sariah had knowingly set an unrighteous example for Laman and Lemuel, they would have been accountable, but that was not the case.

If we had taught our loved ones that suicide was the answer, and our teaching motivated that action, we would be accountable. If we had taught them to turn to drugs and alcohol (if this was part of their problem) and influenced them in that direction, we would have accountability; we would have failed them. But we didn't. We taught them the opposite.

If we had told them *not* to get help for their depression or mental illness (if that was part of the problem) or that mental illness was their fault, maybe we could be considered more culpable. But like most good parents, or spouses or friends, we likely did everything they would allow us to do to help them. We had no control over their choices to abuse drugs or not get psychiatric help. If they did go for help and no medication eased the mental illness, we had no control over that either. None of us had any control over the final act of suicide. *Where you have no control, you have no accountability.*

Blaming Ourselves Is an Exercise in Futility

In the weeks and months following a suicide our minds tend to be barraged with questions. I wondered why I hadn't realized what was going on with Brian in the weeks before his death. He had declined to come to family gatherings and I hadn't seen him for some weeks. I wondered what part of it was my fault. Other questions demanded answers: How could I live with this new reality without losing my mind? What could I have done differently that might have helped? Why wasn't I prompted to rescue him?

Focusing on such futile thoughts can keep us from giving our broken hearts to the Lord—and there really is no other reasonable course, no other way to heal.

My bishop gave me a priesthood blessing that included these words as nearly as I can remember:

> *Listen carefully to what I am about to say because these are the very words of the Lord to you. You should not spend one moment going back and worrying about what you might have done differently. You did everything that could possibly be expected and the Lord accepts that.*

I believe these words apply to most of us in most situations. As parents and spouses and friends we do all we know to do and if we could have done better or more, we would have. Each time I go back in my mind searching for anything I had missed doing, anything that could have made "the difference," I tell myself "Stop! Remember the words in the blessing."

Recently I was told of a suicide where the parents blamed themselves and each other to the point that their marriage and lives were destroyed— three lives were lost instead of one. How useless to compound the tragedy— and compound the pain their departed son was feeling in the spirit world. A counselor also told me of a mother who blamed herself for her son's death and turned inward in grief to the point that she totally neglected her living children. What sad choices that greatly compound the original problem.

When a Suicide Note Casts Blame

We are tempted with inappropriate guilt even when the relationship with the deceased was respectful. But for those who may have the added burden of angry words exchanged before the death, the pain is magnified. An unkind note may have been left with railing accusations against family members or friends. Behavioral Health Specialist, Debbie Bake, who worked in a hospital's Adult Inpatient Psychiatric Unit states:

> *Suicide notes are generally written by those least able to under-*
> *stand reality. Even if a note was written with the intention to hurt*
> *those left behind—with statements such as "I hate you" or "you are the*
> *reason I . . ."—don't give credence to these last desperate words, espe-*
> *cially when you know they were written under the duress of an illness.*
> *Instead, remember the heart of the person who died, the times when*
> *they were not acting out due to factors which may have been beyond*
> *their control.*
>
> *Then, once healing begins, I suggest throwing the note away, along*
> *with any destructive emotions it may have caused.*

You Didn't Cause It!

We are so inclined to get a distorted view of cause and effect in this situation. What I did or did not do was NOT the cause of Brian's suicide. What you did or didn't do did NOT cause your loved one's suicide. The same things we may be seeing as "the cause" are done or not done every day by parents or spouses or siblings or friends whose loved ones never choose suicide. Millions of parents make grievous errors in parenting, yet have children who are still alive. Millions of spouses fail to treat a partner well, yet few mistreated or jilted spouses consider suicide. My perceived failings didn't cause it and neither did yours. And whatever level of influence we may have had, we certainly had no control—nor should we have had. Whose plan was it to control others in order to avoid wrong choices, anyway?

Those attending "Al Anon" support groups—formed by loved ones of alcoholics—are told to remind themselves in regard to alcoholism: "I did not cause it, I cannot control it and I cannot cure it." We can apply these phrases to our own situation. We did not cause our loved one to choose sui-cide. We had absolutely no control over that choice. And we could not cure their problems, whatever they were, that led up to it. (Heaven only knows if we could have, we would have!)

I've thought about what Brian would want for me. Would he want me to blame myself? Would he want me to beat up on myself for not knowing better and not being able to do any more than I did? Of course not. It makes so much more sense to keep my thoughts on the good times. I know Brian would want me to live life to the best of my ability now, to reach out and help others and to enjoy the moment. The more I think about this concept the more it makes sense that the better I do here, the more I help Brian in his progress there. Also, that he is cheering me on. I believe that!

My heart is learning to let go of what I can't control (which is almost everything!), which allows me more energy to deal with what I can control—my own choices, my own thoughts and emotions. The hardest emotion to deal with has been a pervasive feeling of shame.

Confronting Guilt and Shame

I have to admit that my greatest challenge since Brian's death has not been the grief, but getting stuck in guilt and shame. I'm not talking about the Jiminy Cricket conscience thing that would make me think, "Okay, I made a mistake. What am I going to do to make it right?" Or, "I can't fix this. How can I repent so the healing power of Christ can ease my burden?" We all have a conscience that motivates positive change.

However, what many survivors like me have suffered instead is the stuffed down, miserable, self-denigrating, self-blaming, self-condemning guilt not attached to any specific wrongdoing and not resolved by the recognition of God's help to repent. I'm talking about feeling guilty simply because I'm the mother of someone who chose to kill himself, and labeling myself a failure because of this thing I had no control over. Most of what I'm talking about is really "shame."

Shame is damaging because it is a feeling of general unworthiness—not for a bad choice I can repent of, but for a lack of wisdom or spiritual maturity that I think I "should have had." That's like saying "I should know before I have the chance to learn," or "I should perform on a college level when I'm only in kindergarten." God does not require us to do better than we can.

And He gave us weakness so we would turn to Him (think of Ether 12:27). He gave us a Savior because He knew we would need saving!

In a *Meridian Magazine* article called "My Yoke Is Easy and My Burden Is Light," Larry Barkdull said:

> *God programmed the experience of life to be one of continual lack. Our resources and abilities seldom equal what is required to heft our burdens. As we struggle to cope and progress, we find ourselves in the constant need of seeking help from someone who has greater strength and ability. Try as we might, we cannot change life's program. But once we admit that we will never have enough and that we need constant help, we will be in a better position to come to Jesus and draw strength from a Resource that never diminishes.*

The Lord doesn't want us cowering in shame because of our lack. He doesn't want us to despair because we haven't yet become who He knows we will become in the eternities.

Shame is a sinking, doubting feeling about who we *are*. Many, like me, had shame issues long before a loved one died, and now, feeling shame over something we didn't choose perpetuates a cycle of doubt, discouragement, hopelessness, and failure. Think of April's quote at the beginning of this chapter. The scenario of suicide so easily generates shame. In order to protect ourselves against it we must be mindful of the source!

Who Wants Us Stuck in Shame?

It is Satan that wants us to judge ourselves harshly and wrongly. He wants us stuck in misery-producing shame because his desire is for us to become as miserable as he is. The scriptures teach, "Because he had fallen from heaven, and had become miserable forever, he sought also the misery of all mankind" (2 Nephi 2:18). Peter warned, "Be sober, be vigilant; because your adversary the devil, as a roaring lion, walketh about, seeking whom he may devour" (1 Peter 5:8). A loved one's suicide makes us more vulnerable to Satan's wiles, and some days I've felt utterly devoured!

The adversary has had eons of practice to perfect his arts of deception, deceit, despair, and discouragement—all for the purpose of devouring us. We can be sure of the source when we are deluged with feelings of shame. Only the adversary shames us, discourages us, tempts us to give in and give up.

Here's what I think when I'm listening to Satan: *"If I had been a better mother, Brian might still be alive."* I've read that after suicide it is normal to have exaggerated feelings about the ability we *could have had* to influence the one who died. Satan capitalizes on that. He tells us lies that accuse and shame us. One of his names is "the accuser." It's really black and white. When I am in shame, I'm listening to the adversary, and he gets me doubting God's line-upon-line plan which allows me to be human and make honest mistakes and learn and grow at the only pace I can.

Here's what I think when I'm listening to the right voice: *"It's all right to make mistakes—that IS God's plan. Of course I made mistakes with Brian, but those mistakes did not cause his death."* It was Satan's plan to rob everyone of agency *because* agency would inevitably result in mistakes. God safeguarded agency and sent His Son to provide the way to be forgiven of inevitable mistakes so we could be cleansed and able to come back to Him.

The Lord's voice motivates us to keep moving forward, invites us to drink of His "living water." The Savior always sustains and encourages and forgives us. Strangely enough, the Spirit tells me that if I could go back in time I would do exactly the same things in my relationship with Brian. Why? Because I couldn't take what I know now with me; that's not how it works, and I sincerely did all I could with what I knew. The Spirit gently reminds me not to overplay the importance of what I did or did not do. So many other factors entered into the equation.

When a sense of failure or shame begins to settle over me like a dark cloud, I remember that God is on my side and that with His help I can win this battle!

The Battleground Is the Mind

Reading and learning has been essential to my progress. However, I have to stay forewarned and forearmed: Satan works so craftily to turn even the best things I learn against me. With his prodding it is easy to use even gospel truth and understanding to accuse myself. For instance, knowing what I know about the source of shame, I've felt ashamed for feeling shame! Knowing what I know about the source of discouragement and depression, I've been depressed about being depressed! Knowing what I know about the gospel of Christ, I've felt terrible for feeling bad at all! After all, Mormons are supposed to be the happiest people on earth, right? What nonsense to give the adversary such power in my mind.

I believe the true root of sin is to avoid turning to the Lord. Without His help I'm sure to stay stuck in guilt and shame, as well as fear and resentment because I can't deliver myself. But He can! "And none shall deliver them, except it be the Lord the Almighty God" (Mosiah 11:23).

So much depends on what happens in the mind; that is where we must fortify ourselves against the adversary. And that is the subject of our next chapter.

9

The Battleground of the Mind

They cried unto the Lord in their trouble,
and he saved them out of their distresses.

Psalm 107:13

A battle between Satan and the Savior for the souls of men began with the war in heaven and rages to this very day. Much of the battle is subtle and invisible to the eye because it occurs in our minds. Brian's death gave the adversary so much more ammunition to use against me in my mind. Satan, the accuser, who is always determined to "sift me like wheat," stepped up his attacks on my thoughts.

Wait! Satan Doesn't Know My Thoughts

In D&C 6:16 we read, "Yea, I tell thee, that thou mayest know that there is none else save God that knowest thy thoughts and the intents of thy heart." What a comfort! But that doesn't mean that the devil and his cohorts can't whisper thoughts into my mind! The temptations presented by Satan are real and are part of the plan: "Wherefore, the Lord God gave unto man that he should act for himself. Wherefore, man could not act for himself save it should be that he was enticed by the one or the other" (2 Nephi 2:16).

So much of that enticing happens in my mind! Even though Satan doesn't know my thoughts, he knows my weaknesses and tendencies. He knows that because of the fall the "default" setting of my natural man mind is negative. He knows what ploys have worked on me in the past, and he is a master at reading body language. When my shoulders sag and my countenance is dim he knows it's a good time to attack. Satan has absolutely no compassion. He rejoices whenever the blows of life make us especially vulnerable. I have, without a doubt, experienced Satan's attacks more brutally since Brian's death. Other grievers have expressed similar feelings.

Satan's specialty is psychological warfare! If he can turn us in our thoughts against God ("God let this happen and it's not fair!"), against others ("They are to blame!") or against ourselves ("It's my fault!"), we won't have the energy to fight the real enemy—him!

I found the devil and his cohorts constantly whispering thoughts into my mind! We've already talked about many of them. One of Satan's names is "the accuser" and he is well-practiced and accomplished at throwing darts of false accusation. We can recognize his accusing voice clearly in thoughts such as, "You don't deserve to be happy ever again." The temptations presented by Satan to believe his false accusations are real! In no other scenario are we more in need of God's protection and help.

We Are Free to Choose

The good news is this: It is possible to dismiss Satan and choose comfort in the still sweet whisperings of the Holy Ghost. In fact, we have to make the choice constantly. In a wonderful article called "Voice of the Spirit," President Faust indicated that every moment demands that we choose between that which comes from the Lord and that which comes from the devil. Consequently, we choose between the two over and over.[1] I believe that constant choice describes our most basic use of agency. I also believe that a big portion of the stress in our lives comes as a result of resisting or ignoring divine promptings—choosing instead to listen to the adversary's discouraging static.

We *can* choose in favor of the Lord because the mind is the last bastion of agency (as long as one's mind is not fettered with severe mental illness or addiction).

As Viktor Frankl reminds us in his superb book *Man's Search for Meaning*, "Everything can be taken from a man but one thing: the last of the human freedoms—to choose one's attitude in any given set of circumstances, to choose one's own way." Even in a concentration camp where every freedom of action was stripped away, no one could take from the prisoners the freedom to choose their own thoughts and reactions. And no one, not even Satan, can infringe on our agency to choose our thoughts. Like Nephi, we can say, "Rejoice, O my heart, and give place no more for the enemy of my soul" (2 Nephi 4:28).

Most of us would choose against the devil in an instant if we recognized his voice. But he knows precisely how to make his whisperings appealing and reasonable—even tinged with truth—so that we may not perceive that we are in a battle with the adversary at all. While I was working on this chapter, an incredible, faithful woman who lost her son to suicide a decade ago e-mailed me. She stated, as though it were fact, that she was a failure as a mother and that there was no real purpose in her life anymore. From the outside looking in, it is easy to see instantly where those lies come from. She was under attack!

Make Sure Your Reception Equipment Is in Working Order

I don't want to downplay the impact of chemical depression. If implementing the ideas in this chapter does not give you relief from a constant bombardment of negative, debilitating thoughts and feelings, I urge you to seek medical help. When our physical receptors are out of order they simply can't transmit the messages of the Holy Ghost. We literally lose the ability to feel good. Before I got help I wrote in my journal,

"I have this huge emptiness inside. I ache to feel the joy that beauty used to give me. I'm just disconnected from the wonder—but somewhere it must still be there."

Here's the test that works for me: Simply focusing my mind on the Savior, reading His words, thinking of His love and remembering Him, and doing what I know I should opens my personal conduit to the Spirit of the Lord. If it doesn't, it means my body is so depleted or fatigued I can't think straight, or that the chemicals in my brain are out of balance. My friend Debbie told me that when she was in the throes of chemical depression, the more valiant she was in trying to keep the commandments and doing good, the more despair she felt. Why?—because her illness was the cause of her despair, not lack of spirituality.

I've gone for help when I recognized that gloomy, negative, dark feelings did not lift even when I was making the most diligent efforts to focus my mind on good. I've consulted church leaders, professional counselors, medical and alternative specialists. Each contributed something valuable to getting me back on track—whether it was good advice, medication, supplements, or tools for reprogramming my mind. Remember, we do not go for help because of what is wrong with us but because of what is right with us. It makes no sense to struggle on and on with conditions that are treatable; Brian did that. I choose differently!

We Can Win This All-Out War with the Adversary

I have long believed that the war stories in the Book of Mormon are to teach us how to fortify ourselves against the attacks of the adversary. For instance, in the story of Helaman's great battles to defend the Nephites against their Lamanite enemies, we come to a place where they were not receiving the provisions and additional strength to their forces that they badly needed. Helaman's response provides us with an exact formula to follow:

> *The cause why they did not send more strength unto us, we knew not; therefore we were grieved and also filled with fear . . .*

> *Therefore we did pour out our whole souls in prayer to God, that*
> *he would strengthen us and deliver us out of the hands of our enemies,*
> *yea, and also give us strength . . .*
>
> *Yea, and it came to pass that the Lord our God did visit us with*
> *assurance that he would deliver us; yea, insomuch that he did speak*
> *peace to our souls, and did grant unto us great faith, and did cause us*
> *that we should hope for our deliverance in him.*
>
> *And we did take courage . . . and were fixed with a determination*
> *to conquer our enemies. (Alma 58:9-12)*

Let's look at this scripture more closely. First, Helaman said that not
knowing the cause grieved them and filled them with fear. Grief, fear, and
ignorance are such common causes of darkness in our lives. Where did
they turn? They poured out their whole souls in prayer for strength and
deliverance. How many times can I say that I have poured out my whole
soul in prayer? When my son's death shattered my heart I learned more
about this kind of prayer.

Now, in the scripture above, notice that the Lord did not instantly deliver Helaman and his troupes, but He gave them the assurance that He *would*
deliver them. This assurance was all they needed. It brought them peace,
faith, hope, courage, and a fixed determination to conquer.

To "pray always," turning to God in our minds, is our first line of defense. Each morning we need to ask for the Lord's help. As the day progress-
es, we can pray the moment we recognize dark, discouraging, or unworthy
thoughts. *Remember, this is war! We need God's help.*

Joseph Smith set the pattern in the Sacred Grove. He explains, "Exerting
all my powers to call upon God to deliver me out of the power of this enemy
which had seized upon me, and at the very moment when I was ready to
sink into despair and abandon myself to destruction . . . just at this moment
of great alarm, I saw a pillar of light . . ." (JS History 1:16).

God answered and delivered Joseph from the powers of darkness. He
will do the same for us if we call upon Him.

Thoughts Determine Feelings

We walk through an emotional minefield after a suicide. Sometimes we feel totally at the mercy of our tumultuous emotions. There is no more important time to recognize the adversary's lie: "we can't help how we feel." The liberating truth is we CAN help the way we feel because our feelings are tied closely to our chosen thoughts. Satan is well aware of that connection; all the tools in his arsenal tempt us to focus on thoughts that make us feel miserable and undermine our sense of worth and purpose.

Scriptural Examples

I love scripture examples. See the connection between thoughts and feelings in these verses:

> *For when they beheld those that had been delivered out of bondage they were filled with exceedingly great joy.*
>
> *And again, when they thought of their brethren who had been slain by the Lamanites they were filled with sorrow, and even shed many tears of sorrow. (Mosiah 25:8-9)*

Personal Examples

I've experienced the connection between thoughts and feelings so much more vividly since Brian died. No matter how good I've been feeling, all I have to do to plunge myself back into grief and tears is to bring to mind the three representatives of the South Salt Lake Police Department standing by our mailbox, coming to deliver the news that Brian was dead.

All I have to do to plunge into guilt and shame is to entertain thoughts such as, *"If only I could have done whatever would have made the difference. If only I had been more aware and known what was going on, maybe Brian would still be alive."* When I choose a thought that isn't true, the Holy Ghost withdraws, and positive energy leaves as well. When I think, *"I simply can't bear this,"* my energy is drained. When I think, *"I can do all things through Christ who strengtheneth me,"* the Holy Ghost witnesses the truth, and energy flows and light comes back.

I feel so good when I make the choice to bring to mind favorite memories. I can think about sitting at a picnic table with Brian eating McDonald's hamburgers on a sunlit day, watching pigeons swoop down to snatch pieces of the buns we tossed them, or Brian sitting at the end of my bed rubbing my feet and comforting me when I had a bad headache. I can choose to think of my sense of purpose in writing this book! I can choose good feelings!

In no way do I suggest that we can or should avoid feeling our grief. It is a myth that as members of Christ's true church we don't need to grieve because of what we know. Think of President Hinckley's grief after his wife died. Honest grief is healthy. To this day I sometimes cry when I think about Brian's death. Tears are cleansing, softening, healing; I greatly prefer them to being hard-hearted or zombie-like. When I am crying unto the Lord, my heart stays soft, my spirit is teachable, and my sense of gratitude grows.

*Feeling sorrow is not negative—*feeling despair is. *Grieving is not negative—*feeling that I am a failure is. The point is to fortify ourselves not against the sadness, but against the discouragement and false messages of failure. Not against missing our loved one, but against feeling that life is over because they are gone. These are important distinctions! Most of all we need to fortify ourselves against assigning negative and destructive meaning to any of the facts. We can remember that circumstances do not dictate the outcome of our lives—we do!

One of the best suggestions I've tried to follow is to change thoughts of "why me?" or "why did this have to happen?" to "What is required of me now? What can I learn from this? What is it that I need to do today? What is the best choice I can make right now?" I'm amazed at the difference in the feelings those thoughts and questions generate.

One more disclaimer: In no way do I suggest that we stuff negative feelings of any kind. They need to be dealt with. In other places in this book you will find ideas to help process those feelings. I *am* saying that our thoughts matter enormously! I choose how I feel because I choose what I think—and because I have the power to say, "Get thee behind me, Satan" (Luke 4:8) whenever I sense his negative influence on my thoughts.

How This Plays Out in Real Life

After I suggested these principles to a woman named Robin, she e-mailed me back with these comments:

> *Why do I feel so isolated and as if I have been cast off? I truly believe the words you have written to me, but at this point I feel so spiritually beaten up I will have to dig deep to find the energy to put them into action. I want to try—really I do. I am trying so hard not to give up. I feel so alone—obviously, or else I would not be writing to a complete stranger, but I do believe I need to say, "Get thee behind me, Satan." Maybe I will begin with that small statement. I think you are right; I have allowed Satan to convince me I am not a choice daughter of God.*

Robin also posed a question that is common in the midst of adversity. She asked: Will Heavenly Father only help me if I have enough faith? I keep getting stuck in fear.

I replied:

> *I know Heavenly Father helps us when we ask, even if our faith wavers. Remember the man who brought his son to Jesus for healing? He said in all honesty, "Help thou my unbelief." The Lord did, and healed his son. We are in a constant battle in our minds between fear thoughts and faith thoughts and the important thing is to recognize what's going on. The battleground really is in our minds. Whenever the fear comes up, say, "get thee behind me, Satan" and thank the Lord that His power is always greater than Satan's.*

Faith does triumph over fear. I told Robin about an elderly man in our ward who was in a life and death situation—if the broken disk in his neck moved a fraction of an inch one way he would be paralyzed, the other way, he would be dead. Just before he went in for a dangerous operation to insert pins to stabilize his neck, I visited him. As I left, I told him I would be praying for him and that I hoped his operation would be successful. He said, "Whatever happens will be all right. The Lord loves us and that's all I need to know." I was quite awestruck. I really could detect no fear in him. So maybe after the "get thee behind me," we need to add, "The Lord loves me and whatever happens will be all right because the Lord will help me through it."

Thought Patterns Are Habitual, but Change *Is* Possible!

Allowing negative thoughts is habitual (and as I indicated before, the "default setting" of the natural man's mind). But our task is to put off the natural man with the power of the Spirit. I've come to a solemn realization that I have sometimes allowed negative thought habits to get ingrained in my mind—mostly thoughts berating myself. Perhaps because of the fall such thoughts are "natural"—the path of least resistance.

In spite of all the light and truth I've been given, Brian's death has made it much more tempting to fall into the trap of focusing on grief, disappointment, failure, and weakness. Satan tells me that negative focus is being humble, or facing reality, or just owning up to the way things are. But I know better: it is simply his way of pulling me down.

I've learned how important it is to stop the adversary's attack of negative thoughts immediately. I don't know about you, but I have a "downward spiral" that if I don't catch quickly can be like a slide into the pit of discouragement and depression where all I can see is the negative. Sometimes the pattern is simply to obsess about all the things that are not the way I'd like them to be, especially troubling things about other people or the world that I have no power to change!

The first and most important thing to remember is always prayer. In D&C 10:5 we read: "Pray always, that you may come off conqueror; yea, that you may conquer Satan, and that you may escape the hands of the servants of Satan that do uphold his work."

D&C 88:69 warns "cast away your idle thoughts." When negative thoughts surface, I cast them away quickly by using one of the following methods:

1. I de-junk my thoughts by crying out to the Lord, practicing cognitive therapy, or spilling it all out on paper . . . and scribbling over the words, crunching the paper or burning it.
2. I review in my mind everything I have to be grateful for—everything I still have and can still do. I write pages of positives to remind me of good times and faith-affirming events.
3. I say to myself, "I choose the light. I choose the light. I choose the light."
4. I remind myself of God's love by saying out loud, "God loves me."
5. Sometimes I play and sing hymns. (I can even sing hymns in my mind no matter where I am! The hymns have a tangible power to bring the Spirit.)
6. When I sense darkness encroaching, in my mind or out loud I firmly say "STOP! Satan, you are a liar and I won't believe your lies."
7. I put favorite scriptures and thoughts in page protectors to read when I'm in the tub, when I'm resting, anytime. I memorize some so I can repeat them in my mind to displace negative thoughts.
8. At times I visualize Jesus putting a shield of light all around me, protecting me from Satan's fiery darts and lies.
9. I also like to visualize the Savior assuring me that He is aware of my sorrows, righteous desires, of every thought of my heart.
10. Finally, I visualize Jesus holding out His arms to Brian, welcoming him into His embrace

In years past I used to repeat "positive affirmations" about myself in an effort to feel better. Now I know that it isn't about me at all—it's about *Him*. God is who He says He is: He has all power to do what He says He can do. I affirm my dependence on the Lord and His love and mercy. Here's an example of one of my plastic-protected ponder pages I refer to frequently:

The Lord is my light, my source of strength. He is the Way, the Bread of Life, my Counselor, Exemplar, Shepherd. He will guide my thoughts and keep them from anxiety, negativity, and all the temptations of the adversary. May I seek His presence and guidance in all I say, feel, and do. May His light shine on my life and chase away all dark thoughts of fear, doubt, uncertainty, and self-denigration. I choose the light. I love everything to do with light. I love the Lord and desire only to serve Him.

I relinquish my grief to Him. I know His Atonement will heal it all. Faith in God's plan fills me with the opposite of grief. I'm so grateful to know that if there had been a less painful, less grief-filled way to accomplish all the purposes of mortality God would have known and would have implemented it. This life is part of His plan. All our tears will be dried, all our sorrows swallowed up in the joy of the redemption. I relinquish all false ideas I may have inherited to the contrary, all doubts concerning God's goodness, all fears for the future. God rules, the Savior reigns, their purposes are sure and they will prevail! How grateful I am for this knowledge.

I let go of all bitterness over the realities of life and death. No matter how painful, I accept what IS, because it is God's will that all men have their agency to choose how to respond and what to make of their lives. I express thanks for the Savior and His love and redeeming power and caring for each of His children—even me. He will cleanse and purify my heart and help me be His disciple indeed by filling my heart with charity, the pure love of Christ. I'm thankful for life itself and for this day and the choices it offers.

O Remember, Remember

One vital principle for thought control is choosing to remember the doctrines of Christ and all the positive witnesses of the Spirit that we receive. Recently I read in my journal two experiences of supreme significance that I had, to my complete amazement, entirely forgotten. I recounted them in

Chapter Two; they documented times the Spirit told me that Brian had been taught, and had accepted Christ.

I found these journal entries the very last month I was finalizing this book. Some of the things I wrote before were tentative on this very point because I had forgotten! How could I forget something so vital, so comforting?

Since the first printing of this book I found yet another entry that I had totally forgotten that gave me great joy, dated August 26, 2008: "Friday night Doug and I both had vivid dreams about Brian. I dreamed that he told me he had read all my articles and wanted me to write for him because he wanted to get on the airways and tell people what he had been learning. Amazing. We both thought Brian appeared happy and well when we saw him in our dreams."

We deprive ourselves of so much strength and joy when we neglect to record, re-read, remind ourselves of the great spiritual moments of our lives. Surely it is one of the adversary's best devices to snatch away these moments of pure light from our remembrance and get us to focus instead on current frustrations or past grief. I've started a special file of spiritual times I don't want to forget—one I can find easily and refer to frequently.

Keeping Our Minds Focused on Light and Truth

In Jacob 4:13 we read, "For the Spirit speaketh the truth and lieth not. Wherefore, it speaketh of things as they really are, and of things as they really will be; wherefore, these things are manifested unto us plainly, for the salvation of our souls. But behold, we are not witnesses alone in these things; for God also spake them unto prophets of old."

Recognizing the voice of the Spirit in our minds can have a positive impact in our lives as we focus on it and follow promptings. Recent general conference talks have been replete with this message. Also, in the April 2010 Saturday morning session of General Conference, Sister Julie B. Beck indicated that the ability to qualify for, receive, and act on personal revelation is the single most important skill that can be acquired in this life. Her whole talk, which I highly recommend, focused on the significance of this principle.[2]

It became clear to me why taking the Spirit as our guide is so vital when I read D&C 45:56-57, which defines the wise virgins in Jesus' parable as "they that are wise and have received the truth, and have taken the Holy Spirit for their guide, and have not been deceived—verily I say unto you, they shall not be hewn down and cast into the fire, but shall abide the day."

We need that guidance! Our minds need that light so we won't be deceived. The Gift of the Holy Ghost is a constantly renewable source of strength, light, and truth. Through the Holy Ghost we can win the battleground of the mind!

Light Prevails

D&C 98:3 states, "All things wherewith you have been afflicted shall work together for your good, and to my name's glory, saith the Lord."

Even Brian's death? How could it be? But the Lord gives no exceptions to "all things." It is not that Heavenly Father caused it; quite the opposite. As I've noted before, so many who have either attempted suicide or been tempted to, have stated that they experienced a literal barrage of thoughts in their minds telling them that death is the only answer, that everyone would be better off without them, and on and on. There is absolutely no doubt that the adversary is involved—and Satan's work is so much easier when a brain is dysfunctional. Illness may be the root source of the problem, but the devil takes advantage of a weakened mind. One thing we know for sure: when suicide happens, the devil's will is done, not the Lord's.

However, the Lord takes even this heart-wrenching situation and brings good from it *if we will let Him.* He reminds us that the Atonement covers not only sin but also the grief resulting from every error in judgment, weakness, and lack in ourselves and others. The Lord wants us to feel happy, to know joy in this life and hereafter. How it is possible, even now?

Years ago in a presentation about grieving, I heard Deanna Edwards say, "Joy is not the absence of pain, but the presence of God." Those words entered my heart in a powerful way and keep coming back to me in this situation. No matter the pain, the presence of God brings an assurance of

His love, which is "the most desirable above all things . . . and the most joyous to the soul" (See 1 Nephi 11:22-23).

When I feel the Spirit, and my thoughts are focused on Christ and His love for me, all is well, no matter if the whole world is in chaos. For that very reason I have felt joy and a greatly increased sense of gratitude and well-being while I've been working on this book. No wonder the adversary tries so hard to keep us from focusing our minds on the Lord and feeling His Spirit with us. He doesn't want us to feel that joy. But light always triumphs over darkness in the end.

The Lord has given us the formula for winning the battleground of the mind in so many scriptures, such as the following: "Look unto me in every thought; doubt not, fear not" (D&C 6:36); "Let all thy thoughts be directed unto the Lord" (Alma 37:36); "Let virtue garnish thy thoughts unceasingly" (D&C 121:45). I'm sure you have your favorites that have strengthened you.

In my journal I recorded what my bishop said to me a few weeks after Brian died:

> *Anytime a feeling of hope comes up, capture and hold onto that feeling. Hope doesn't come from the adversary, but from the Lord. Ask the Lord in any moment of pain to apply the healing blood of the Savior. Listen to the Lord's messages to you personally, believe them and follow them; give yourself credit for your willingness and for your good desires. Remember the Lord's great love and mercy and that He is undoubtedly giving Brian the fullest measure possible, leading him lovingly to belief and to access the Atonement in his behalf.*

When I follow my bishop's counsel and turn my thoughts continually to Christ, I feel good. We CAN help how we feel because we CAN choose how we think. With the Lord's help we CAN cast Satan out of our thoughts, choose to focus our thoughts on the Savior and His mighty power to save. When a room is dark and we open the drapes and let the sunshine in, the darkness flees. But when a room is full of light and we open the drapes and it is dark outside, the light does not flee. Light rules over darkness. Christ has power over Satan, but Satan has no power over Christ. Regardless of the outer circumstances, Christ is ready and willing to fill our minds and lives with His light. He will give us the joy of His redeeming love.

Remember 2 Timothy 1:7, "For God hath not given us the spirit of fear; but of power, and of love, and of a sound mind." We have been promised, "Thou wilt keep him in perfect peace, whose mind is stayed on thee: because he trusteth in thee. Trust ye in the Lord for ever: for in the Lord JE-HOVAH is everlasting strength" (Isaiah 26:3-4). He will help us be among those "whose mind is stayed" on Him if that is our sincere desire. With His help we can win the wars waged on the battleground of our minds.

Notes

1. James E. Faust, "Voice of the Spirit," *Ensign*, Apr. 1994, 8.

2. See Julie B. Beck, "And Upon the Handmaids in Those Days Will I Pour Out My Spirit," *Ensign*, May 2010, 11.

Reclaiming
Life

And there arose a great storm of wind, and the waves beat into the ship, so that it was now full. And he [Jesus] was in the hinder part of the ship, asleep on a pillow: and they awake him, and say unto him, Master, carest thou not that we perish? And he arose, and rebuked the wind, and said unto the sea, Peace, be still. And the wind ceased, and there was a great calm.

Mark 4:37-39

10

Let's Not Get Stuck in Grief

We glory in tribulations also:
knowing that tribulation worketh patience;
And patience, experience; and experience, hope.

Romans 5:3-4

It is no surprise to learn that grief is ongoing, but we don't want to get stuck in it. The hard part is giving ourselves time and permission to feel it when it comes up. Keeping busy is good, but we need to safeguard time alone when we can acknowledge our feelings. In my journal, dated December 29, 2004, I wrote: "I'm so shut down, but I don't want to sit around and cry, either. I'm sick of crying, but when I avoid it for very long I get so miserable I have to let the grief out. How does one appropriately grieve?"

It took me a long time to find answers to that question. The next three chapters document what I've learned, such as the importance of spending some thinking, feeling, processing, and praying time alone whenever I'm able to get up early.

I e-mailed my friend Ann, who was grieving the loss of her mother, sharing how important early morning alone times had become to me. She replied:

> *Your pre-dawn quiet time sounds like such nourishment. I enjoy the sense of throwing my whole self into a project, but when I'm involved, I'm not aware that my grief cup is slowly filling. I seem to be made in such a way that I must pause occasionally and acknowledge the cup, and feel my pain. Only then can I move on with a lighter heart. I've been doing some of that today. Sometimes it's hard to go as deep as the pain is—it's scary to find it so alive, still pulsing and red, even after so many visits into the "pain dungeon." Knowing that the anniversary of your son's death is approaching, it must be hard. Do be gentle with your dear self.*

Finding Time to Grieve

Grief is a matter of the heart, not the head. I've heard that logic can never open a door that emotions have shut. I've found that it is vital to knock on the door of my heart and see what is going on there. (In the next chapter I detail the writing therapies I use to accomplish that task.)

The most common pattern as life's demands keep coming at us is to use activity to escape feeling. We think we can escape the pain by simply staying too busy to think about it. I had the best of excuses to stay over-busy at first. My daughter-in-law threatened early delivery and was put on bed-rest three days after Brian's funeral. She and my son had four little boys seven and under. Grandma was needed. I did an academy award-winning recovery, put my grief aside, and functioned because I needed to (and maybe because I was hoping it would be an eraser for my pain). But sometimes the energy it took to hold in all the grief made me so tired I could hardly move.

After the birth of the baby in November, the flurry of the Christmas season somehow kept me busy and distracted until January. I was stuffing my grief and not even acknowledging that it was there. Finally, in January, the grief and depression I had held at bay overtook me and I found myself crying nonstop. This time I couldn't escape it or cover it up—and it was too big for me to deal with. I wrote in my journal, "I feel like an empty shell, a blah bag of nothing. I can't imagine ever feeling enthusiastic or excited about anything again."

I knew I was in trouble and went for medical help. For the short term, an antidepressant gave me some stability so I could function . . . *and* so I could quit procrastinating the final awful task of ordering Brian's grave marker, which was symbolic of the whole thing—a final admission that Brian was gone, that I had to accept his death and deal with it. Doug was so sweet to me as I tried to work through my feelings and muster the courage to walk back into the funeral home. He built a fire in the fireplace and let me talk it through until the tears finally came.

I had a hard time accessing *any* of my feelings as soon as I began taking an antidepressant. I hadn't been feeling much at all, and soon found that I preferred feeling honest grief to not feeling at all. A nurse likened medication to a bandage that covers an emotional wound. When it is sufficiently healed, you carefully remove it. I know that many people aren't this lucky, but I was grateful when, just over a year later, I was able to remove the bandage, stop taking the medication, and feel more like myself again.

In the meantime, I still made significant progress at grief work—two steps forward and one step back, but it was progress because I was starting to uncover and admit how I really felt.

We Can Get Stuck in Grief by Ignoring It

We may try to reason ourselves out of grief, but it won't work. Grief is emotional energy, and energy is indestructible. When feelings are not acknowledged, they go underground, but they don't disappear. They may fester like an infected sore. What are the results of ignoring our feelings?

Emotional Problems

Some sources say that most emotional problems (as high as 80%!) are rooted in grief gone underground.[1]

Physical Problems

One reason that grief work is so important is that unexpressed grief can manifest itself as physical ailments—such as immune deficiency disorders, chemical depression, stomach problems or frequent colds. I have Chronic Fatigue Syndrome (CFS) and frequent illness from the Epstein Barr virus. Attacks are triggered by stress, emotional turmoil, and overwork. Needless to say, when I ignore my feelings, the turmoil increases. The enormous energy it takes to stuff down, hold in, deny feelings, and act as if everything is fine robs me of the energy I need to function and stay well . . . it makes me sick! It also keeps me from the wisdom that can come from dealing with my trials openly. Oh, how I've needed to feel my grief in order to keep my health. I've had to learn to acknowledge my sorrow, lean into it, and work through it, instead of running away from it.

Behavior Problems

Stuffed grief also manifests itself in behavior changes—such as becoming a workaholic, losing ourselves in excessive sleep or TV watching, or social withdrawal. We can get stuck in grief by ignoring it.

And, the more grief we stuff, the more it accumulates, the more our health suffers from these ineffective traditions of stuffing emotions. We can become like a volcano about to erupt. Simply put, when not acknowledged, grief undermines both emotional and physical health.

Why Do We Stuff Our Feelings?

First, life doesn't provide "time off" for grief work. Maybe you work full-time or have small children that keep you busy more than full-time. It may not be easy to find even an hour to focus on and work through your feelings, but it's important!

Secondly, society doesn't teach us how to deal with broken hearts. And neither do most families. Most of us have been encouraged to bury our feelings, keep a stiff upper lip, act strong so others don't break down. Functioning from the head and not the heart is more "efficient." We are told to keep busy, so we bury ourselves in work and refuse to think about our grief. When we try to unwind at bedtime, sad thoughts flood in and disturb our sleep. No wonder we get so tired!

Third, so many tasks, demands, and entertainments distract us from the actual grief that needs to be dealt with. It's more convenient and comfortable to ignore our own emotional turmoil as well as that of others and get on with the tasks at hand. We are a very task-oriented society after all. So many of those tasks involve technology, which is anti-feeling. A recorded voice message doesn't care how you feel. The computer doesn't care how you feel. And even most people "out there" don't have time to care. After a tragedy it's more comfortable for the people around us if we don't show our emotions or talk about what happened.

Acknowledging Feelings Is the Key to Progress

Being willing to feel our real feelings can be the key to the breakthroughs. Distraction only works for the short term. We want relief and resolution in the long term. There is authenticity in pain; ignoring it is ignoring part of who you are.

What I'm calling "grief work" is often seen as a waste of time. But it's essential for healing parts of ourselves we may not even know are broken. Grief presents all of us with grief-work tasks. Emotional health is about choosing to do these tasks, even though it requires time. I can't over-stress how important it's been to me to spend time admitting how I feel and being really honest with myself—partly because the idiom "time heals all wounds" is a lie. Time heals nothing. Only doing the grief work and being willing to receive healing from the Lord can heal all things. The Lord beckons us to "lie down in green pastures" to rest and heal. In those green pastures we can acknowledge our feelings and vent them. That must occur before healing can happen. Stuffing doesn't work.

Wayne Brickey, author of *Making Sense of Suffering*, pointed out the need to draw ourselves apart and take time for our grief when he said: "Suffering places us behind a door and hides us somewhat from the view of others. The privacy allows adjustment, renewal, and transformation. The fortunate interruption allows us to break old chains."[2]

Jim Miller has created a website called Grief and Loss—Willowgreen, Inc. (www.Willowgreen.com) that offers online help, including books, tapes, and videos for those who are grieving. Look for his list of 48 "Grief Tips"—for those who mourn. He says, "All wounds heal the same way— from the inside out. The best way to handle your feelings is not to 'handle' them but to feel them."

Think about your own patterns. How much do you stuff your feelings? If you do this a lot, is it because you simply don't know what else to do? The next chapter details the "how to's" of grief work.

Notes

1. See *Grief Recovery Handbook* in the Resource section of this book.

2. Wayne Brickey, *Making Sense of Suffering*, Deseret Book, Salt Lake City, Utah, 2001, 10.

How to Do Grief Work

*I will turn their mourning into joy, and will comfort them,
and make them rejoice from their sorrow.*

Jeremiah 31:13

Grief work is a matter of appropriately expressing rather than stuffing feelings. Some of the simplest suggestions I've received have proven to be powerful healing tools. When I've made the choice to feel and express feelings in appropriate ways, my progress has accelerated.

Here are suggestions that have helped me to express rather than stuff feelings. I hope some of them will help you too:

1. Cry When You Need to Cry; Venting Is Vital
2. Find Safe Places to Talk about Your Grief
3. Set Aside Time Each Day to Grieve
4. Use Writing Exercises

Cry When You Need to Cry; Venting is Vital

I've come to believe in the importance of feeling my feelings. There is a cleansing, strengthening power in tears. I like the Jewish proverb that says, "What soap is for the body, tears are for the soul."

I usually like to cry alone. However, especially in the immediate aftermath of Brian's death, crying with others—raw sorrow shared—forged stronger bonds of love, and there was some relief in mutual expression of our grief. Every person I've cried with I've drawn closer to. I find a sense of being human and alive in my grief as long as I am honestly expressing it and allowing others in to share their grief with me. Tears can keep the pressure inside from building up and becoming unbearable. The hardest times have been when I couldn't cry. Grief can still sneak up on me, like when I hear one of the songs sung at Brian's funeral; and I still find the need to cry occasionally. It provides a safety valve; a vent.

Sometimes I feel more like screaming than crying, and that too, can be a good release—screaming until the emotion is spent. I've tried that a few times when I'm home alone, and it helps!

Sometimes I find hitting a punching bag or pounding a pillow good venting strategies. Other times, I found the most help in safe places to express my feelings verbally.

Find Safe Places to Talk about Your Grief

We all need to find a place to openly express feelings without being judged or having others trying to fix us. I was referred to a grief support group provided by a national organization called "Caring Connections, a Hope and Comfort in Grief Program." (See contact information in the Resource section.) About five months after Brian's death, my daughter-in-law and her new little baby accompanied me to six weekly meetings. I was so glad for this outlet! We were given a manual, lots of helpful handouts, and a memory book to write in about our loved ones who died by suicide. Most importantly, we were given a chance to share with others who understood.

A founder of a support group called "Wings" said: "It was a safe place to express our true feelings and to question. We asked each other 'Why?' We shared the guilt we felt that we didn't recognize the precarious state our loved ones had been in and that we hadn't been able to protect them. We shared our frustration at not being able to change things. We shared the thoughts, books, articles and scriptures we each had found helpful. Most of all we listened to and encouraged one another."

Such groups, often headed by trained grief counselors, offer a safe and appropriate place to meet with others who are in a similar situation. It's good to talk and be listened to sympathetically, to empathize and feel empathy. If you happen to attend a group that is not supportive and helpful, don't hesitate to back away and try other resources.

Banding together with others who have suffered a similar loss eases the dreadful feeling of aloneness. We need to vent, and to hear from others who are still breathing and have survived this awful experience. Telling our story (talking *or* writing) gives context to grief and can decrease both its intensity and duration. Sad and angry feelings need to be appropriately expressed! If you can't find a support group, at least find a caring family member or friend who will let you talk as long and as much as you need to.

Family and friends can be our best "support groups." My childhood friend, Gayla Wise, who had recently lost both her parents, referred me to the *Grief Recovery Handbook* (see Resource list for full information). She also walked me through a lot of the exercises the book suggested and which I describe later in this chapter. We cried a lot of tears together and found the process very therapeutic. Gayla and her caring, sturdy friendship helped me through the grief enormously.

My best friend, Patricia, had lost a brother-in-law to suicide and was always there for me, always ready to lend an empathetic ear, as was my dear sister Arlene. I don't know what I would have done without them because within a month of Brian's death I felt that no one else around me wanted to talk about the whole sad experience—and I still very badly needed to talk!

We need each other! Paul taught, *"Bear ye one another's burdens, and so fulfil the law of Christ"* (Galatians 6:2). I'm so grateful for those who e-mailed me in response to *Meridian Magazine* articles I wrote about Brian. They could not have given me support if they hadn't known about my plight. We have to let the right people know! I cannot underestimate the helpfulness of feeling supported and not being alone in this. Brenda Floyd was one of the first, and she has continued to contact me over the years. Her understanding and support (having been through the ordeal herself) have been invaluable.

Set Aside Time Each Day to Grieve

An LDS psychologist, Russ Seigenberg, who lost a daughter to a drug overdose, used his training to develop techniques to help him deal with his pain, guilt, depression and grief. He explained that the procedure which made the most difference was The Hour of Contemplation. He set aside one hour a day to grieve and focus on the emotions and problems he was dealing with. At the same time he made an agreement with himself that the rest of his day he would concentrate on the other concerns of his daily life. He said:

> *My subconscious, or inner self, seemed to view the idea of grieving an hour per day as an ideal solution. I had already worked through my guilt feelings and so it was more of a loyalty issue. Setting aside a time to grieve immediately resolved the conflict I had been feeling between holding onto the grief longer and feeling guilty or disloyal if I let go of it. My depression just vanished. I had never before recognized that emotions were so closely connected to the thoughts of the subconscious. I now tell people that whenever they are feeling emotions not tied to conscious thoughts, that their subconscious is processing something.*

I read somewhere that the highest tribute we can pay to the one who died is not continued grief, but gratitude for the time we had with them and the love we shared. That grief is part of the price we pay for loving (where there is love, there is pain), but we don't have to pay that price forever. Grief is a process. Recovery is a choice.

Use Writing Exercises

As mentioned earlier, writing about feelings can be therapeutic. I often write about the type of feelings I can't talk about. Writing therapy has helped me to admit, access, and vent feelings.

Whenever I can, I get up early when the world is quiet and the phone is *not* going to ring, and just write—whatever comes up. Occasionally I ask myself pages of questions; later on, answers may pop into my mind.

I've found Cognitive Behavioral Therapy (CBT) to be helpful. I write my negative feelings in one column and in the other column what my heart tells me could also be true or truer than my original belief. (See additional information on CBT in the Resource section.) Another exercise is to write down negative feelings and sort through them. I see which ones I can do something about, which are irrational and need to be let go of, and which are in the category of "just needing to be accepted." Accepting the unacceptable, as in the case of suicide, seems impossible. Robynn said:

> *The first thing I had to do was accept what had happened. I had to ask myself what was I supposed to learn from the situation. There was obviously a lesson in this for me; what was it? I also had to stop the "what if's." The reality of the situation is that what was done was done, and no matter what I did, it wasn't going to change the fact that he was gone. When I made a conscious decision to accept what I could not change, I was able to shift into a space where I could learn and grow.*

I've found real acceptance possible only with the Lord's help. Writing helps me reconnect and feel that help. I often talk to the Lord on paper and find Him answering me. A good spiritual exercise is to write a favorite scripture verse, ask myself how I feel about it, how I could apply it, and see what comes up. I believe that it's not only my subconscious that can speak to me through my writing, but the Holy Ghost, as well. Feelings are often the bridge across which the Spirit must pass to comfort and strengthen us. If we choose to keep our feelings locked inside the castle of our hearts, if we pull up the bridge, and create a moat to keep others out, we may also inadvertently keep the Holy Ghost out.

Specific Grief Work Exercises

During my grieving process I learned that we can restructure relationships with loved ones—even after they are gone. How? Writing exercises are one of the best ways. The most helpful I've found are detailed in a book I highly recommend, *The Grief Recovery Handbook* by John W. James and Russell Friedman. The authors summarize an effective process for healing from any kind of loss.

The authors suggest that undelivered emotional messages, coupled with feeling incomplete in a relationship, keep grief going. I will summarize the exercises that best helped me unlock my emotions and deal with my grief. (More detailed explanations are, of course, found in their book.)

Create a list in chronological order of what you consider the greatest losses of your life. (I didn't really want to do this, but took a deep breath and wrote two pages—starting with loss of health because of a severe burn when I was tiny, and ending with Brian's death.)

Create a relationship graph. Draw a line down the middle of the page. Beginning with your earliest memories, jot in the left column the saddest things you remember from your relationship and on the right the highlights and happy times. (In the left column I started with a sad moment when Brian was two and ended with my grief when I learned he had chosen to leave this life. In the right column I listed the highlights, the happiest events, like birthday parties, family trips, and heart-to-heart talks.)

List anything you feel you need to forgive. (I listed things like Brian's passive-aggressive tendencies.)

List anything you need to be forgiven for in the relationship with the loved one lost. (I listed things like my over-programmed life that left me so little time to focus on him.)

Write any undelivered emotional messages you wished you had been able to communicate. (For instance, I wrote out how much I wished he could have known how much I loved him all his life and how much I wanted to be his friend.)

Write a personal letter to your departed loved one, then read the letter out loud as though you were reading it to him or her. (I found this process especially helpful, and somehow felt I was really communicating to Brian.)

I did these exercises over a period of a week and found them extremely helpful. Anything we talk about or record on paper seems more manageable and less threatening or anxiety-producing. Much of the feeling of having "unfinished business" with Brian dissipated after I completed the assignments. One of the things the writing helped me recognize is that an event has zero meaning until I assign it one. I really can choose how to feel and how to respond to Brian's death, as well as anything else that has happened.

Continuing the Process

Some of the exercises, like writing letters to Brian, I continue to do at intervals. I often give myself time to write and reflect on "anniversary" days. Writing letters to Brian often feels soul-cleansing. Here are some excerpts of the letter I wrote to Brian at the five-year point:

Dear Brian,

Five years ago, sometime during the night you had the experience of being ushered into the world of spirits. I wonder what it was like for you. I wonder if you were amazed to learn how much you were really loved. I wonder how you felt about your life as you looked back on it. I know there were many good things—helping friends, listening to friends—that I know little of. I know you tried to be true to yourself, honest with how you really felt and that your friends valued that honesty. So did I. I told you once that I wanted to be more like you when I grew up—in those ways. You seemed surprised, even startled.

What was it like for you when you were taken home to the God who gave you life? Did you immediately learn that Jesus was the Lord? Did He greet you personally? Did you feel the Savior's love for you right away? I know He knows you and loves you. I love you so much and I don't know a fraction of what He knows about you.

What is it like there for you now? How much progress have you made? There should really be nothing to hold you back. You have an environment of perfect love and truth. You have so many progenitors on both sides of the family who were stalwart souls. Surely they care about you. How does that all work on the other side, anyway?

Do you play your guitar and romp with your dog Sheba, or are you too busy learning, and perhaps even teaching others by this time? You don't have to eat or sleep or do any of the chores that are necessary here, so I wonder what life is like on a daily basis. Do you have days and nights? Do you go to classes or teach classes? Do you do service projects for people on earth? Are you a guardian angel to any of us down here? Are you in a dimension where you constantly know what is going on with us, or do you get only an occasional glimpse? Do you know when I am having a hard time? Does the Lord let you visit whenever you want, or only on special assignment? I know I can't have the answers to all these questions, but I wonder because I love you! Mom

Writing is a powerful tool; it has played a major part in my quest to regain emotional and spiritual strength. Anything we talk about or record on paper seems more manageable and less threatening. And much of the feeling of having "unfinished business" with Brian dissipated after I had completed all the writing exercises on the list.

Seeking Help with the Process of Grieving

We all need help. As I said about depression: We don't go for help because of what's wrong with us, but because of what's right with us. It's healthy and good to recognize when we don't have all the resources we need to get better. There is so much we need to learn! It's good to look for and find support groups, counselors, books, tapes, classes—whatever meets your needs. (Check the Resource section for a whole list of websites, books, etc.) It's good to get help in communicating with your spouse and other loved ones. That ability to communicate is even more vital in a situation like this.

For dozens of more specific helps for grievers and those who are supporting someone in grief, see the charts of Do's and Don'ts in chapter thirteen.

12

Grief Has Purpose

They that sow in tears shall reap in joy.
He that goeth forth and weepeth, bearing precious seed,
shall doubtless come again with rejoicing,
bringing his sheaves with him.

Psalm 126:5-6

The Lord had purpose in providing for opposition in life's experiences. I suspect that if joy and sorrow, bitter and sweet, light and darkness could simply be explained to us, our loving Heavenly Father would have spared us the difficulty of experiencing them. But only experience seems to "get through" to us. Perhaps we are inclined to learn so much through difficulty and sorrows because in the midst of them we are so inclined to turn to the Lord. Psalm 118:5 reads, "I called upon the Lord in distress: the Lord answered me." Years of talk about sorrow could not teach as much as one minute of experiencing it. Nothing teaches like experience.

Grief Is Our Teacher

We've all heard that this life is a school. If that is true then loss and grief must be among the toughest classes in that school! Since the beginning of time people have suffered not only because of their own wrong choices, but also because of the poor choices of those around them, and because of the death of loved ones. However, there is purpose in every part of the plan, even the pain. Brigham Young said, "There is not a single condition of life that is entirely unnecessary; there is not one hour's experience but what is beneficial to all those who make it their study and aim to improve upon the experience they gain."[1]

Elder Orson F. Whitney is often quoted saying that no pain that we suffer or trial that we experience is wasted—and he lists all kinds of reasons why.[2]

In 2 Nephi 2:2 we read, "Thou knoweth the greatness of God; and he shall consecrate thine afflictions for thy gain." I stand amazed as my comprehension of the "gain" from afflictions increases. I see that only such adversity is likely to motivate me to mighty prayer. I see that my suffering has propelled me to seek the Spirit, and repent. It has been the means of my choicest experience with the power of redemption. It has given me a great desire to be instrumental in turning others toward that redemption.

Grief Has Pain, but Also Promise

My friend, Mary Smith, wrote me:

> *Grief is like the ocean—calm and peaceful, and then a wave starts to rise [higher and higher until it] breaks over one like a tsunami. The pain, the self-examination, the doubt, the tears all begin again. The wave subsides and so does the power of the grief until the next time. However, each wave gets a tiny bit smaller and the time between waves grows longer until one day you realize you have gone an hour and then two between the pain and the promise.*

What is the promise Mary speaks of? I believe it is the power of the Comforter, the light of truth, the power of soul growth and acceptance.

So many of us who have suffered the loss of a loved one through suicide have wondered if we could ever smile again, ever feel joy again.

As long as we don't turn away from the Lord, the answer is always a resounding "Yes." Author Robert L. Veninga said, "Once you have experienced the seriousness of your loss, you will be able to experience the wonder of being alive. It is a fact that once you experience pain, it sensitizes you to joy."

Yes! I'm sensitized to joy. I appreciate it more for the rare commodity it is, and treasure it when it sneaks up on me. How can I explain how much more I feel of life, how much deeper and more meaningful my life experiences seem since I suffered the heart-wrenching loss of my son? Lord Byron said, "Sorrows are our best educators. A [person] can see further through a tear than a telescope."

Bruce C. Hafen explains in his book, *The Broken Heart,* that the moments of our greatest stress and difficulty may be the very times when the refiner's fire is doing its best and most purifying work.[3]

My experience validates those words. I also seem to be recapturing pieces of myself that I had lost long before my son's death. It's like I've been invited to examine faulty assumptions, and restructure experiences that led me to those assumptions. I recognize in a deeper way how much better life can be when lived in light and truth.

In short, my grief has been the bud that has blossomed into spiritual joy. In 2 Nephi 2:23 we read, "Having no joy, for they knew no misery." I know misery, all right, and have experienced how opposite it is from joy! Note the account of Ammon and his brethren in regard to their missionary work: "Their sufferings in the land, their sorrows, and their afflictions, and their incomprehensible joy" (Alma 28:8). There is a vital link between affliction and joy.

Silver Linings

In the early weeks after Brian died I wrote:

> *All through the difficult, tear-stained days, I have had a deep inner sense of blessings beginning to bud and blossom—things I have prayed*

for fervently over the years beginning to be fulfilled. I am inclined to cry out:

Oh Father, I wanted a broken heart and a contrite spirit—but not this way! I wanted to feel progress in the cleansing of my heart; I wanted to know firsthand the power of the Jesus' saving grace for me and for my loved ones—but not this way! I wanted closer family relationships, to have heart-to-heart talks with family and friends, to be able to give and receive the pure love of Christ—but not this way! I wanted to raise my voice in pure testimony of the reality of the Savior's love and His intercession on our behalf—but not this way! I wanted a closer connection with the afterlife, to be able to sense its reality and have greater hope for spiritual help—but not this way!

However, I realize that "my thoughts are not your thoughts, neither are your ways my ways, saith the Lord" (Isaiah 55:8). Little do I understand the ways He fulfills His purposes in my life. He grants men freedom of choice and honors it at all costs—but when those we love make decisions that wrench our very heartstrings, He is mighty to fulfill His promise that "all things shall work together for your good" (Romans 8:28).

There is good reason that "The Lord *is* nigh unto them that are of a broken heart; and saveth such as be of a contrite spirit" (Psalm 34:18). A broken heart lets go of the cares of the world like a broken vase relinquishes the water that filled it. When our heart is broken we relinquish distractions, worries, mental distress, and confusion—and focus on listening to His voice. We let go by trusting the Lord that we will be taken care of and that we will be able to do the one thing that is needful. We believe the Psalmist's words, "Cast your burdens upon the Lord, and he shall sustain thee" (Psalm 55:22). We develop the ability to feel his watchful care in every situation, every adversity. What greater blessings could we ask for? Always look for the silver linings—bursts of light that break through even the darkest clouds!

Cherish the Gifts That Come with Grief

The universality of grief comes largely because of the universality of love. Love and grief are opposite sides of the same coin. One of the best lessons I've learned is to tell others today that I love them; we must not wait for a tomorrow that may never be. It's easy to shower my grandchildren with love, harder to tell grown-ups, but it's important to do it. One never knows when a fleeting opportunity to express love could be the last in this life.

From Jim Miller's *Willowgreen* website I gleaned the following ideas, which I share with his permission:

> *Your sadness is real, yet it need not be final. While it brings you pain, it can also bring wisdom and strength. From it you will learn secrets about yourself and truths about others. You have known deep joy before; you can yet again. Despite your brokenness, and somehow even because of it, wholeness awaits you. Despite what you have lost, and somehow even because of it, you stand to gain. You hold the possibility of experiencing life with a maturity and a compassion and appreciation you have never known before. So be open.*
>
> *Know that the life which flows through you has been given as a sacred gift. Cherish that gift. Nurture it. Above all else, hallow the preciousness of each passing moment that is yours, for this is where the miracle of life resides, and this is where you must go to find it.*
>
> *Finally, remember that your destiny was predicted by the writer of the Book of Job: "You will forget your misery, you will remember it as waters that have passed away. And your life will be brighter than the noonday; its darkness will be like the morning. And you will have confidence, because there is hope."[4]*

Yes! There is hope! Remember, healing does not mean finding a quick cure, but putting the loss in perspective. We reclaim our lives by feeling our feelings and by gaining glimpses of an eternal perspective in regard to our loss.

I've always loved the last verses of the hymn, "How Firm a Foundation"—

the ones we hardly ever sing, but that have such a powerful message. Written by John Rippon in 1787, they resonate in my current situation, especially the following:

> *When through the deep waters I call thee to go,*
> *The rivers of sorrow shall not thee o'erflow.*
> *For I will be with thee, thy troubles to bless,*
> *And sanctify to thee thy deepest distress.*[5]

Notes

1. Brigham Young, *Journal of Discourses,* 9:292.

2. See *Improvement Era*, March 1966, 211.

3. Bruce C. Hafen, *The Broken Heart*, Deseret Book, 1998, 97.

4. Excerpts from the conclusion to the Willowgreen videotape, *Listen to Your Sadness: Finding Hope Again after Despair Invades Your Life:* by James E. Miller.

5. *Hymn from the Oremus Hymnal Wiki,* verse 3.

13

Do's and Don'ts for Grieving

Helpful Guidelines for Grievers and Those Who Love Them

The following lists have been compiled from many sources, including my own experience. The first list gives Do's for you, the griever. The second gives Do's and Don'ts for anyone who desires to support and help someone who is grieving.

Of course, you the griever are also going to be in the position of helping others who are grieving, so the second list is really for you too. Offering support to others simply means letting them know we care. Sometimes we can best do that just by silently being with them. It doesn't mean healing or curing or changing things; but staying near in the face of grief, despair, confusion, and powerlessness. Most of all it means accepting and loving.

Do's: For the Person in Grief

Do **let yourself grieve as much as you need to.** Don't believe that if your faith and trust in God are strong you won't grieve. Don't assume that you should be able to snap out of it, go on with life and not worry because your loved one is with God and you know you will see them again and they will be resurrected. Academy-award recovery doesn't work. Grief is valid and real and inescapable and needs to be felt.

Do **let your emotions out!** What we resist persists. Talk, share your tears and your feelings and learn from them—cry, read, listen to music. Acknowledge your feelings and don't stuff them. Avoiding pain is not the answer. Feeling it and working through it is.

Do **answer questions truthfully with your minor children.** You need not hesitate to say, "I don't know" if you don't. Let children speculate about the unknown without judging their words or ideas. Take time to talk to them and listen to them. Let them be involved. It helps them to better understand what has happened.

Do **get help.** Don't believe that reaching out to others for help shows weakness. It takes strength to reach out for help. You go for help because of what's right with you, not what's wrong.

Do **let your grief take as long as it takes.** There is no timetable for grieving and no one else can tell you how to do it. Listen to your heart and follow your instincts and the Spirit!

Do **give yourself permission to grieve in any way that feels right to you.** Don't compare your grief with someone else's or downplay it. Grief, like all wounds, heals best from the inside out. There is no "right" way to grieve. The many natural disasters resulting in massive loss of life may make you feel small for thinking your grief is so big, but you can't compare your grief with the grief of others. You are entitled to your pain over this particular loved one, even if thousands just died in some natural disaster. There is no such thing as better reasons than yours to grieve—and we all grieve at one hundred percent for us. Your grief is just as valid as anyone else's, not more or less so.

Do **expect to keep missing your loved one.** The grief work may come to an end, but the missing won't. Celebrate their life through memories.

Do **take care of yourself.** When you are grieving it is all too easy to let all former good health habits go to the wind. The first few days after a tragedy, self-care is, understandably, the furthest thing from your mind. However, for obvious reasons it needs to become a priority again—quickly! Remind yourself that you need to be gentle, patient, encouraging, and forgiving to yourself. Give yourself permission to do things you love, things you do well. Even the smallest accomplishment will help.

Do **exercise.** It will help you unwind from tension, work off bottled up feelings, and get tired enough to sleep well. Sometimes even the exercise of pounding a pillow if you're angry can help bring back equilibrium and calmness. Exercise stimulates circulation, improves the lymphatic system, and gets more oxygen to the cells. Exercise makes you feel better and can loosen the hold of depression when you feel down. So many times depression is anger turned inward. Letting feelings out, even in physical activity, can decrease depressed feelings. The word "depressed" means held in, held down, kept from flowing. Physical movement gets things flowing. It's good to stop what you're doing at least every hour and stretch and exercise a bit to get your circulation going again. Even two minutes of exercise can make a big difference!

Do **practice deep breathing.** Breathe deeply at intervals—in the car, at the computer, etc. Whenever you think about it take a few good deep breaths. Deep breathing stimulates physical energy. You think more clearly when you breathe deeply. Deeply inhaling, then blowing the breath out with vigor is a good way to decrease negative emotions and toxins. (I read that seventy percent of toxins are eliminated through the lungs!)

Do **pay attention to what you eat.** Good nutrition is vital, even to support emotional healing. When you eat what's good for you, you are being your own best friend. Be nice to yourself by eating food that not only tastes good, but also gives you the nutrition you need. Try, for instance, mixing a smoothie in the blender with pineapple juice, a little spinach and parsley, a squirt of flax seed oil, and frozen banana and other fruit to taste. Avoid white sugar and white flour and too much fatty meat. Stay away from soft drinks, tobacco, alcohol and drugs. Eat whole grain breads and cereals, eggs, steamed vegetables, salads, sprouts, etc. The more you eat what is good for you, the less you will care about or even want what isn't. You might consider it a form of fasting to abstain from foods you know are not good for you. Such "fasting" makes you more likely to function on a higher level—not just physically but spiritually.

Do **make uplifting music a part of your routine.** Nothing soothes the nerves and lifts the heaviness in the heart more than good music. For example, try listening to whatever music seems to soothe your soul. Two albums of memorial songs have been created to provide comfort to people after the death or suicide of someone close. (To find this music, just Google "Before Their Time," vols. 1-2.) Deanna Edwards has also created music that is specific to give uplift to the grieving. The right kind of music invites the Spirit and makes it easier to keep thoughts positive.

Do **relax when you need to.** Good books on tape can be helpful. Focusing the mind on something that edifies helps avoid obsessive thoughts and encourages relaxation. There are many good relaxation tapes available. "Journey to Peace" with narration by Nancy Hoskins and piano music by Paul Cardall is a superb tool for relaxation. It is Christ-centered, full of assurance of God's love, and includes many scriptures. It helped me more than any other one thing. Also Google "Brain Healthy" music by Paul Cardall such as *Be Calm: Sleep Music by Paul Cardall*, which includes a relaxing nature video.

Do **take soothing baths to aid relaxation.** Try adding Epsom Salts or ginger for cleansing, or lavender oil for its soothing qualities (and other various essential oils). Aromatherapy is wonderful and can relax and nourish both body and spirit.

Do **share the following list of Do's and Don'ts with friends and family.** Please follow them yourself as you interact with others who are grieving.

Do's: For Supporting the Person in Grief

Do **say:**

- I care. I love you. May I hug you?
- It must be difficult. Remember, I'm praying for you. (It is possible to experience a tangible *feeling* of being cushioned by the prayers of friends.)
- I can't imagine how hard this must be.
- Would you like to talk about ___? (Just to hear the name of your loved one spoken respectfully can be incredibly sweet.)
- Do you remember when . . . ?
- Please come to dinner tomorrow.
- Let me take your kids for the afternoon.
- I would be angry too.
- You don't have to hide your tears. Thank you for sharing them.
- I don't know what to say, but I love you and I'm here. You are not alone.
- I loved them too.
- What I'll always treasure about _____ is _____.
- I'll never forget the time he _____.
- It's okay; I'm happy to listen. Tell me again about _____. [Nothing hurts more than wanting to talk about your loved one and being greeted by silence. Talking is healing.]

- I just phoned to say hello and that I care.
- The anniversary day may be tough for you. Can we spend it together?
- I thought you might need some company today. May I come visit you?
- I love to _____ (mow lawns, make spaghetti, trim bushes, etc.), may I do it for you?
- I was so sorry to read about your loss (if you found out about the death in the obituaries). Would you like to talk about it?

Do **give hugs and show genuine love and concern.** We all need love and affection and warmth. A random act of kindness is always appreciated.

Do **use the name of my loved one who died.** Share good memories about them if you knew them.

Do **let me cry, be angry and upset.** There are only a few people I can open up with who still want me to talk about this tragedy.

Do **call and initiate times to be together.** Just being there for me shows caring even if you don't do or say anything.

Do **let me talk.** Be willing to listen without interrupting. I may have an almost insatiable need to pour out my feelings.

Do **allow for silence and tears.** Do cry with me if you can.

Do **try to understand me.** Let the Spirit guide and direct you to know what can be done to help, because while I'm grieving I may not even be aware of my own needs.

Do **come to my home** and say, "I'm here to do whatever needs to be done." I would never ask, but oh, how welcome it would be if you just showed up with suggestions of what you are willing to do, such as shop for groceries. (I'll pay, of course, and give you a list of what I want.) Offer to cut the grass if it's summer, shovel the snow if it's winter, rake the leaves if it's autumn, wash the windows if they need it, do a batch of laundry, or run necessary errands. Drive carpool if I'm supposed to, or if I have small children offer to take them for a few hours. I especially need breaks from that responsibility right now.

Do **remember that your presence alone may be what I need.** You don't always have to do something. Just having someone care enough to be with me can be one of the best comforts.

Do **remember the grieving of my minor children.** They might appreciate a separate card or note addressed just to them. They might need you to talk to them alone. According to their age, they might appreciate one of the following: bubbles, play dough, sidewalk chalk, a Frisbee, water colors, gel pens, markers, movie tickets, a pizza, ice cream, gift cards, and support in their sports, hobbies, and studies.

Don'ts: For Supporting the Person in Grief

Please *Don't* **avoid me.** Nothing can hurt more than that.

Don't **tell me you know how I feel.** If you haven't been there, you have no idea what it is like. Even if you have been there, no two situations are alike.

Don't **tell me how I should feel** or how I should be responding to this situation.

Don't **tell me I'll get over it** and everything will be back to normal again.

Don't **set a timetable** for when I should be through grieving.

Don't **compare my situation** with anyone else's or try to convince me it could be worse.

Don't **ask too many questions or make judgments;** I'll feel them even if you don't voice them.

Don't say:

- They're in a better place.
- Try not to think of them.
- Just think happy thoughts.
- You need to get on with your life.
- Aren't you through grieving yet?

Be patient with me, please. Grief is not orderly or predictable, AND it takes time—sometimes a REALLY LONG time. In the meantime, the most important thing we can give another is attention. Just being there, sitting with me, sometimes in loving silence, can have more power to heal and connect than the most well-intentioned words.

Rebuilding on Christ, the Rock

Remember, remember that it is upon the rock of our Redeemer, who is Christ, the Son of God, that ye must build your foundation; that when the devil shall send forth his mighty winds, yea, his shafts in the whirlwind, yea, when all his hail and his mighty storm shall beat upon you, it shall have no power over you to drag you down to the gulf of misery and endless wo, because of the rock upon which ye are built, which is a sure foundation, a foundation whereon if men build they cannot fall.

Helaman 5:12

14

How the Refiner's Fire Purifies Our Beliefs

When through fiery trials thy pathway shall lie,
My grace, all sufficient, shall be thy supply.
The flame shall not hurt thee; I only design
Thy dross to consume and thy gold to refine.

"How Firm a Foundation"

Can anyone doubt that the suicide of someone we love is a kind of refiner's fire? No event in my life has ever caused me to re-think what I believe as much as this one. As a practicing, believing Latter-day Saint, my identity was intertwined with "forever family" goals and "I am a child of God" ideas. I felt challenged at every turn. Platitudes and formulaic answers didn't help. Gratefully, my searching and reaching has allowed this refiner's fire to clarify my thinking about many things. In this chapter I'll focus on only a few.

Faith, Prayer and Agency

So many of my friends have children who have strayed for years but are back in the Church and doing great now. Brian never came back into the Church and now he is dead. The hardest question I faced was: could the outcome have been different for Brian if I'd been a better person, if I'd had more faith, if I had been more effective at mighty prayer? The "ifs" were suffocating. Sometimes I felt I was left with only two choices, neither of them positive:

1. To condemn myself for not having what it takes to draw on the powers of heaven to help my son—(after all, look what happened when Alma the Elder prayed for *his* son). Or:

2. To be angry at God for the seeming injustice of it all. (If it *wasn't* my lack that was to blame, then God must not be as impartial as He proclaims Himself to be. The Lord has, in answer to prayers, saved so many others—even from attempts at suicide—why not Brian?)

Over time I've recognized that Alma the Younger and the Sons of Mosiah (and even the rescued children of others) are actually the exception. Consider Adam and Eve—surely as faithful parents as ever lived—and their grief over Cain's choices. Think of the prayers and righteous example of Lehi and Sariah; yet, Laman and Lemuel continued to rebel.

Agency is the ruling law of heaven; the strongest parental faith cannot over-ride it. I received an e-mail from a woman who said, "From someone that has attempted suicide, know that suicide is a personal choice, and only the one that chooses it can lay claim to it. Brian would take full responsibility for his choice."

I know that. When we cleaned out his apartment, a printout on his wall said, *"Responsibility is a unique concept . . . You may disclaim it, but you cannot divest yourself of it. Even if you do not recognize its presence you cannot escape it. If responsibility is rightfully yours, no evasion or ignorance or passing the blame can shift the burden onto someone else."* - Admiral Hyman Rickover

I wrote in my journal, "I feel those words apply to this situation. Brian would not want anyone else to feel even a shred of responsibility for his decision. He would take full responsibility for it."

I also take full responsibility for my own choices . . . for anything I need to repent of . . . for how I'm choosing to respond to this present challenge . . . for how I'm choosing to re-evaluate my life and thoughts. My experiences have changed my perception of so many things—especially what pleases the Lord.

Rethinking What the Lord Really Wants from Me

I used to think that the Lord wanted me to work hard enough and be a good enough mother that I could present my sons to Him as practically perfect people. Because I was living with that paradigm, Brian's exit from church and family activity and foray into drug and alcohol abuse wiped me out. I remember my feelings of failure when Brian's picture appeared in the Salt Lake Tribune after they interviewed him in regard to one of his jobs—as a bar tender, and again, not many years later when I sent the write-up and his picture for the obituary section.

I had done my best and it hadn't been good enough. The worst had still happened. Totally unable to maintain any semblance of the Molly Mormon image, I found myself depleted in every way. I couldn't keep up the pace and I couldn't keep up the façade. I didn't even want to. I had to find a better way.

The Pain of Unrealistic Expectations

In my head I knew perfectly well that my youthful expectations had been unrealistic. But part of me still hung onto the ideal. Here's how it goes: By "choosing the right" I expected to create a home where every true principle was taught and exemplified with effective clarity, where both parents were paragons of virtue, full of gospel goodness and love for each other . . . where every day was a Spirit-filled exercise in gospel living and gospel joy . . . where each child's every need was met so they could go forth from that home filled with strength and testimony ready to make the world a better place.

That picture sounds so pie in the sky, yet I had been completely taken in by it. And every Mother's Day for decades I had grieved over the cavernous gap between that ideal and the reality I lived with. Wasn't it about time I

133

exchanged that unrealistic picture with a solid scriptural-based view of the real purpose of mortal experience and the real responsibility of parents?

What Is Reality?

What I previously sought, without realizing it, was either a Garden of Eden experience for my children—where everything was beautiful and pleasant and we walked and talked with God—or a city of Zion or celestial experience here and now without the testing and proving time necessary to get there. Was I totally forgetting the law of opposition and the necessity of adversity?

The reality is that Adam and Eve were cast out of the Garden of Eden and no parents on this earth can re-create it in mortality. Their posterity, including me and my children, live in the lone and dreary world, the same of which the Lord said, "cursed is the ground for thy sake; in sorrow shalt thou eat of it all the days of thy life; Thorns also and thistles shall it bring forth to thee" (Genesis 3:17-18).

Mortal life is simply not planned to be easy! But the thorns and thistles are for our good: the Lord said He cursed the ground *"for our sakes."* Our job as parents is *not* to create a place of comfort and lack of challenge for our children. Of course we'd never plant thorns and thistles in the ground of our children's lives on purpose, but we can be sure there will be some. No matter how hard we try to smooth the way, our children are going to have trials and adversities. That is God's plan.

The Lord has said, "My people must be tried in all things, that they may be prepared to receive the glory that I have for them, even the glory of Zion; and he that will not bear chastisement is not worthy of my kingdom" (D&C 136:31). But of all our trials and chastisements we are told, "*all* these things shall give thee experience, and shall be for thy good" (D&C 122:7).

Building celestial character traits is our goal, but celestial conditions are not possible in this telestial world. And the experiences of this sphere are calculated to bring us to our knees in humble recognition of our need for the Atonement and our need for constant spiritual guidance. Our problems and trials show us our lack, and our lack is designed to motivate a closer walk with the Lord. (See Ether 12:27.)

The Homes We Are Born into Are Part of God's Plan

One of the biggest struggles I've had since Brian's death is questioning the Lord for placing Brian in our home which He knew perfectly well was going to be so imperfect! What I have come to grips with is that the Lord has perfect foreknowledge of what will happen in the homes in which He places each child. An all-knowing God has tailor-made the resulting trials to teach each child the exact lessons he needs to learn. Neal Maxwell said:

> *The truth about foreordination also helps us to partake of the wisdom of Alma, when he said we ought to be content with things that God has allotted to each of us. (See Alma 29:3-4.) If, indeed, the things allotted to each were divinely customized according to our ability and capacity, then for us to seek to wrench ourselves free of every schooling circumstance in mortality is to tear ourselves away from matched opportunities. It is to go against divine wisdom, wisdom in which we may once have concurred before we came here and to which we once gave assent.*[2]

The implications of those words are breathtaking. It seems that less-than-perfect parents (and spouses and children), and difficult and challenging home circumstances are part and parcel of the testing and trying of this probationary experience. God knows exactly what He is doing when He places each child in each home. He never makes mistakes. His placements inevitably give individuals the precise difficulties they most need for their particular personality in order to fulfill their particular mission on this earth. Who am I to say that Brian did not (or will not, in the eternities) fulfill his?

So many times it is not *in spite of,* but *because of* difficult home situations that people develop the strength of character and drive to become who the Lord wants them to become. For example, how many people do you know who have developed their best characteristics in a Herculean effort to do things differently from the way their parents did them?

Turning Our Hearts Over to the Lord

As I moved ahead, I began to ponder more about the whole experience, and dig deeper. Just what was I learning or supposed to learn and why? Stripped of all ability to be the "shining example," I began to recognize how prideful that need had been in the first place, and how much I had misunderstood basic doctrines. The refiner's fire was line upon line purifying my beliefs as well as my heart.

My friend Sheila e-mailed me:

> *We need to turn to the Lord completely. Only His help in these last great and dreadful times will suffice. I am so saddened by the number of sisters that I write to who have not found the Lord at all, even though they have attended every meeting, taught every lesson in their callings, and are still lost in feeling worthlessness, despair, and lack of spirituality. I believe that "lengthen your stride, do more, work harder, fill each second with busy-ness" is melting away to be replaced with "be comforted, these are days of trials, seek the Lord, be still and know that I am God." The Lord is with you and will never leave you. With His help you can endure to the end.*

Self-condemning thoughts are from the adversary, not the Holy Ghost. They are a temptation, not the truth. They are evidence of Satan trying to turn me from my course, trying to rob my joy. Over and over it was like the Savior was saying to me: "I want you to come and let Me love you. I need you to feel stillness and be nurtured and healed. I want you to let go of the pride that has kept you wanting to look good. I want you to turn it all over to Me and just let Me bless you."

Turning things over to the Lord *takes practice*. When I said that to my e-mail friend Becky, she responded:

I think you've hit on something. Turning things over to the Lord seems to take LOTS of practice. My biggest problem has been that when I have thought of "turning it over," IT tends to be whatever the issue or situation is. What I really need to turn over to Him is my heart. Won't the rest fall into place if I do that? I know I would have to keep doing that, because it is my nature to take it back again. Proverbs 3:5-6 a "let go and let God" scripture: "Trust in the Lord with all thine heart; and lean not unto thine own understanding. In all thy ways acknowledge him, and he shall direct thy paths."

Becky is right. What the Lord really wants is my whole heart—and He wants it broken.

A Father's Poignant Words

There are as many scenarios that break our hearts as there are people. The Oviatt's situation, for example, was very different from mine. I can't imagine what it was like for them during the years their daughter, Laura, repeatedly attempted suicide and all their efforts to help her find relief from her mental illness came to naught. Dee sent me the words he spoke at his daughter's funeral and gave me permission to share them with you. I think they summarize the combination of grief and hope that most of us have experienced.

In the gospel of John is related the death of Lazarus. As you remember, after learning that Lazarus was sick, Christ did not immediately go to him. When he finally arrived in Bethany, Lazarus had already died. First Martha, then Mary approached the Savior and said to him, "Lord, if thou hadst been here, my brother had not died" (John 11:21). Today in my heart I say, "Lord, if thou hadst been here, my daughter had not died. Where were you? Why weren't you here?"

And how did Jesus reply? To Mary and Martha he said, "Thy brother shall rise again . . . I am the resurrection, and the life: he that believeth in me, though he were dead, yet shall he live: And whoso-

ever liveth and believeth in me shall never die. Believest thou this?" (See John 11:23-26.) I do believe this. To me and my family, the Lord says, "Your daughter and sister Laura will rise again. Though she is dead, yet shall she live." This is my hope.

As the Savior approached his own death, he said to his apostles, "Let not your heart be troubled, neither let it be afraid" (John 14:27). Because of her severe mental illness, Laura's heart was very troubled and afraid for most of her short life. I have hope that she is finding the peace that escaped her in this life.

I also have hope in God's mercy. In a passage from the Book of Mormon, the prophet Alma teaches his son that "mercy cometh because of [Christ's] Atonement; and the Atonement bringeth to pass the resurrection of the dead; and the resurrection of the dead bringeth back men into the presence of God; and thus they are restored into his presence" (Alma 42:23). I have hope that Laura is with God and that God is comforting and loving my daughter.

In the atoning sacrifice of Jesus Christ is found the hope that I seek. We lived in God's presence before we were born here. In this life, out of God's presence and walking by faith, we are tested and tried, and we grow and learn and struggle and triumph and love . . . and sometimes experience great pain. We draw on the blessings of the Atonement to know that Christ overcame death and hell for us, that he knows us, that he loves us, and that he helps us in our trials. And after this life we will return to his presence to be, as described by the prophet Nephi, "encircled about eternally in the arms of his love" (2 Nephi 1:15). This is the plan of salvation or, as it is sometimes described in scripture, the "great plan of happiness" (Alma 42:8). I have hope that Laura is encircled in those loving arms and is happy.

A psalm teaches us that "the Lord . . . will be a refuge . . . in times of trouble" (Psalm 9:9). I have hope for this help in the difficult days ahead. When I cry out in my heart, "Where are you, Lord? Where is the refuge in my time of trouble?" I will be comforted by the passage from another *psalm, "Be still, and know that I am God" (Psalm 46:10).*

In 2 Samuel, when King David learned of his son's death, he said, "O my son Absalom, my son, my son Absalom! would God I had died for thee, O Absalom, my son, my son" (2 Samuel 18:33). Today I cry out in my heart, "O my daughter Laura, my daughter, my daughter Laura. Would God I had died for thee." Jesus Christ did die for my daughter Laura. And in the end all will be made right for her and for us. Someday we will be reunited with Laura.

Thank you, Heavenly Father, for the privilege of knowing and loving Laura. How honored I am to have been her earthly father. Please take good care of her. I love you, Laura.

Dee's daughter was a person who exemplifies the fact that gospel understanding and living a righteous life doesn't preclude suicide. I've talked to parents whose sons graduated from seminary and institute, went to the temple, served missions, yet still were snared. These parents were setting excellent examples. Their righteous actions do not give a guarantee of safety from the refiner's fire. We are all left to turn to the Lord's promises for comfort.

Elder George Q. Cannon, a member of the Twelve in the early days of the Church, said these comforting words:

No matter how serious the trial, how deep the distress, how great the affliction, He will never desert us . . . We may pass through the fiery furnace; we may pass through deep waters; but we shall not be consumed nor overwhelmed. We shall emerge from all these trials and difficulties the better and purer for them, if we only trust in our God and keep His commandments.[3]

Trials are so much more intense if we compound them with dismay at God, questioning His love and goodness. Yielding ourselves to the Lord and His will may seem risky, dangerous. However, I've come to believe that trusting God *no matter what* is the only safety we have.

Somehow, some way, we are given motivation to trust God enough to turn our lives over to Him. It's an amazing process, actually—how the very things that cut us down to nothing carry the potential to build us up to what the Lord wants us to be. The Refiner's Fire does us a great service when it purifies our hearts as well as our beliefs.

Notes

1. Verse 4 in the online version—*Oremus Hymnal Wiki.*

2. Neal A. Maxwell, *Things as They Really Are,* Deseret Book, Salt Lake City, Utah, 1989, 31.

3. George Q. Cannon, *Collected Discourses,* 2:185.

15

Forgiving Ourselves and Feeling Christ's Forgiveness

And now, the plan of mercy could not be brought about
except an atonement should be made;
therefore God himself atoneth for the sins of the world,
to bring about the plan of mercy.

Alma 42:15

*I*n Luke 4:18, 21 we find Jesus reading Isaiah 61 to a Sabbath congregation: "The Spirit of the Lord is upon me, because he hath anointed me to preach the gospel to the poor; he hath sent me to heal the brokenhearted, to preach deliverance to the captives, and recovering of sight to the blind, to set at liberty them that are bruised." Then He closed the book and said, "This day is this scripture fulfilled in your ears."

I have, since Brian's death, found myself in each of the categories Jesus mentioned: I have been brokenhearted, captive to fear and negative thoughts, blind to the truth, bruised in mind and spirit. Through the whole experience, the reality of Christ and His promises has been seeping into the crevices of my broken heart. I find that the most important thing is to stay open to hope. The opposite—hardheartedness—is a condition I want to avoid at all cost.

Earlier in this book I've talked about forgiving others and forgiving the one who died. Now I conclude by talking about forgiving ourselves and personally feeling the Lord's forgiveness. I wrote in a letter to Brian about my continuing need to repent and feel forgiven:

> *Oh Brian, sometimes I feel that my heart is still full of wounds. Will it ever be healed? I'm still feeling the need to know that you forgive me, Brian. The last thing in all the world I ever wanted to do was to hurt you in any way, but I know I did sometimes. I only wanted to be there for you and to help and encourage you. You are so dear to me. Bone of my bone, flesh of my flesh. I'll never forget the joy I felt when you were born. I had the absolute knowledge that I had known and loved you before, that this was a reunion. I so look forward to the next reunion when all the shackles of mortality will have fallen off, when we can see each other in light and truth without all the discomfort of misunderstandings and lack of communication. I must not jeopardize that reunion by not forgiving and being forgiven. Perhaps forgiving myself is the hardest part.*
>
> *What do I need to do to allow the Lord's healing to take place? Sometimes I've gone around numb because I didn't have the physical strength to deal with the emotional hurts any longer. I want to live with open loving. I don't want to live behind walls, holding in the pain, not letting others in. I want to feel the Lord's love and let the love spill over to others.*
>
> *The Lord is blessing me in spite of my many shortcomings, Brian. I feel His Spirit leading and guiding and comforting me so often. But I still feel I am living far below my privileges in that regard—that if I did my part better I would feel so much more love and guidance from Him.*

I have a great desire to repent and do better.

I need the Lord's Atonement in my behalf. I need the atoning blood of Christ to cleanse me from my errors in judgment, my pride and self-righteousness, my tendency to judge myself and others harshly. I need forgiveness in so many ways; I am trying to work out my salvation in fear and trembling. I feel such an assurance that you are too. Can we help each other? Your loving mom

Forgiveness Just IS

I remember one day I was praying hard to understand how to know my repentance had been accepted. I was yearning for peace of mind about this whole situation with Brian, and the impact of my imperfect choices on him. The answer I received was that I just needed to accept the promises of the scriptures, period. If God says it, it is true! He will deliver. God cannot lie. And God's scriptural promises apply to everyone. I am not the exception. Brian is not the exception.

Enos set the example when he prayed for forgiveness. He heard a voice saying, "Enos, thy sins are forgiven thee, and thou shalt be blessed" (Enos 1:5). Enos didn't question the Lord; instead, he gave his testimony in these words: "And I, Enos, knew that God could not lie; wherefore, my guilt was swept away" (v. 6). It really is that simple. It is the adversary, not the Lord that would have me linger in unnecessary guilt after I've repented.

But hadn't I heard since my childhood that no other success could compensate for failure in the home? And here I was with a record of divorce and a child who had died by suicide. I cried with relief when I read Elder Bruce C. Hafen's words: "Sometimes we say that no other success can compensate for our failures in the home. And while it is true that no other success *of ours* can fully compensate, there is a success that compensates for all our failures, after all we can do in good faith. That success is the Atonement of Jesus Christ. By its power we may arise from the ashes of life filled with incomprehensible beauty and joy."[1]

Forgiveness Is a Choice, Not a Feeling

I've mentioned this concept before, but it is so important I am going to say it again in different words. The Lord's forgiveness and the power of His Atonement does not depend on my fickle feelings. No matter how I feel, no matter my level of ability to forgive myself at the moment, the eternal promises of the Atonement are true.

Our feelings can be distorted, warped, just plain wrong. Self-pity is self-imposed. When we accuse God of being absent, it is more probable that *we* are the ones not showing up.

Writer and editor, Maurine Proctor, said the following in a *Meridian Magazine* article:

> *Our emotions, however intently we feel them, can lie. It is the earthbound natural man talking, not the eternal, ancient spirit who sees so much better.*
>
> *If we have felt to sing the song of redeeming love, then it is our privilege to live with resolve, no matter how we feel on a given day or a given hour (since our feelings can change just that rapidly). Just now we are too tired, too sick, too sorry, too mad, too worried, too dull to care. Still, we have stood forth as one who has decided, without glancing back, to be forever on his team, bound to him by covenant and therefore, bound to find him.*

We don't have to feel a certain way to make the words of Christ true. *They just are.* Feelings are affected by fatigue, what we eat, physical problems and diseases, hormones, mental problems, thought distortions, grief, depression, and more. But the truth stands firm regardless of our feelings. *I can choose to simply accept the fact that the Atonement is in effect in my life. The Savior's promises are true and apply to me as they do to every living soul who accepts Him and comes to Him.*

I don't need to ruminate about how forgiveness works or *if* it works in my particular case. I am no exception. There are no exceptions to the forgiveness offered after sincere repentance. I certainly haven't committed the unpardonable sin—and neither have any of the people I need to forgive. The Savior's arms are extended to all of us. When I accept His offer I can know His Atonement IS being applied in my life. That's all there is to it.

I've learned as fast as I could. I've changed as fast as the Lord has seen fit to show me my weakness and given me the strength to do differently. In my journal, written October 24, 2005, I wrote, *"My heart has truly been broken as I've recognized how many ways I let my children down without realizing it—but maybe that recognition is part of the plan. A broken heart and contrite spirit is required as our offering; it is necessary for salvation."* Psalm 34:18 says, "the Lord is nigh unto them that are of a broken heart; and saveth such as be of a contrite spirit."

Yes, I am full of weaknesses and shortcomings. But the Atonement covers not only sins, but also inadequacies, errors of judgment, ignorance and imperfections. God has forgiven me for my sins of ignorance and is strengthening me in my inadequacies. I can forgive myself too!

We All Need the Atonement Every Day

No matter how diligent I may have been and am trying to be now, I continue to fall short; consequently, repentance is always part of the journey. The scriptures clearly mark the path. Consider Alma's powerful words: "I thank my great God that he has given us a portion of his Spirit to soften our hearts . . . And I also thank my God, yea my great God, that he hath granted unto us that we might repent of these things, and also that he hath forgiven us . . . and taken away the guilt from our hearts, through the merits of his Son" (Alma 24:8, 10).

The counsel is clear: come to Christ and seek His Spirit, His grace, His forgiveness—and *believe His words*. If we ever find ourselves guilty of believing *in* Christ without *believing Christ* (His words and His promises to us), Stephen E. Robinson's book *Believing Christ* offers exquisite examples and clear words to help us over this hurdle.

The Promise of the Atonement Is at the Center of the Gospel

In his superb talk "Broken Things to Mend," Elder Holland said that reliance upon the merciful nature of God is at the very center of the gospel Jesus taught. He testifies of the depth and breadth of the Atonement in such a beautiful way. Be sure to look this article up and read it. It is so comforting.[2]

One day I got the distinct impression that Brian was helping me on this book and that somehow the tremendous effort of its creation is part of the Lord's healing, redemptive process for both of us. As I've proceeded, always seeking the Lord's help, my focus on what I've learned from all this has clarified my thinking. It has also increased my recognition of my continuing need to repent—and of the Lord's outstretched hands and willingness to help me. Most of all I've seen how central the Atonement is in our teachings, and how easy it is to find evidence of it.

As I've proceeded, the hardest thing has been choosing between literally hundreds of scriptures and testimonies and witnesses of His reality and Atonement. Everywhere I look I see more!

O Then, Is Not This Real?

I have always loved the passage in Alma 32 where Alma teaches the process of coming to a knowledge of truth by trying an experiment of the word, planting the seed, nurturing it, and observing "that it hath sprouted up, that your understanding doth begin to be enlightened, and your mind doth begin to expand" (v. 34).

But verse 35 has always reached out and grabbed me most: "O then, is not this real? Yea, because it is light, and whatsoever is light, is good, because it is discernible, therefore ye must know that it is good." I bear my own personal witness that it is real! Christ was born. Christ lives today. His Atonement is our one true hope.

The story of Christ's birth, life, death, resurrection, Atonement, and love for us is real, full of light, discernible. The absolutely best thing that has happened to me through this trial is coming to a deeper sense of His reality. I feel that reality burning deep in my bones this minute.

Building Our Foundation on the Rock of Our Redeemer

If I could put into one sentence what I have experienced and what I have heard from others who have walked this path it would be this: The most valuable result of adversity is personal experience with the love of God and the Atonement of Christ.

Brenda Floyd said:

> *In these few years since Danny's death, I have come to know personally the power of the Atonement. Believing, not just believing IN my Savior. Truly He is my Personal Savior—for grief is very personal. The suffering that refines me is part of my path back to Him. I tightly hold the words of the Prophet Joseph Smith close to my heart: "All your losses will be made up to you in the resurrection provided you continue faithful. By the vision of the Almighty I have seen it."*[3]

In Helaman 5:12 we read, "Remember, remember that it is upon the rock of our Redeemer, who is Christ, the Son of God, that ye must build your foundation; that when the devil shall send forth his mighty winds, yea, his shafts in the whirlwind, yea, when all his hail and his mighty storm shall beat upon you, it shall have no power over you to drag you down to the gulf of misery and endless wo, because of the rock upon which ye are built, which is a sure foundation, a foundation whereon if men build they cannot fall."

The devil sent forth his mighty wind when suicide ripped through our lives like a tornado. His hail and mighty storms beat upon us. But we know our one Source of hope. Not even this great grief will have power over us to drag us down to the gulf of misery and endless wo if we build on the only sure foundation: the rock of our Redeemer.

So many scriptures talk of the storms of life and give reassurance that the Lord will see us through them all. Here's another of my favorites: "You know, brethren, that a very large ship is benefited very much by a very small helm in the time of a storm, by being kept workways with the wind and the waves. Therefore, dearly beloved brethren, let us cheerfully do all things that lie in our power; and then may we stand still, with the utmost assurance, to see the salvation of God, and for his arm to be revealed" (D&C 123:16-17).

When I read those words I am led to praise the Lord for His plan, for the Comforter that has kept me sane, for the scriptures that daily feed my soul and remind me of sweet spiritual promises that can still be mine.

I can now say, with Alma, "Therefore, let us glory, yea, we will glory in the Lord; yea, we will rejoice, for our joy is full; yea, we will praise our God forever. Behold, who can glory too much in the Lord? Yea, who can say too much of his great power, and of his mercy, and of his long-suffering towards the children of men? Behold, I say unto you, I cannot say the smallest part which I feel" (Alma 26:16).

We Are in the Hands of God

The Lord has given so many scripture promises, such as, "Yea, they shall not be beaten down by the storm at the last day; yea, neither shall they be harrowed up by the whirlwinds; but when the storm cometh they shall be gathered together in their place, that the storm cannot penetrate to them; yea, neither shall they be driven with fierce winds withersoever the enemy listeth to carry them. But behold, they are in the hands of the Lord of the harvest, and they are his; and he will raise them up at the last day" (Alma 26:6-7).

I can't read the words "they are in the hands of the Lord of the harvest" without finding tears of gratitude. In the introduction of my book *Trust God No Matter What!* I tell the story of a dream I had several years before Brian died that has given me great comfort ever since. I feel impressed to repeat it here:

> *A few years ago I was going through a hard time spiritually. One night I had an unusual dream—so real, so vivid. I saw myself driving alone up a narrow mountain road, shivering in the cold of a dark, rainy night. Fear enveloped me. The road had no shoulder, no place I could turn around or pull over, much as I wanted to. I was driving slowly, care-*

fully, higher and higher up the mountain, but the road was treacherous and slick with rain. As I approached a hairpin curve I suddenly realized I could not hold the road. I've never been more terrified as my car sailed off into black, dark nothingness. I was falling, helpless, knowing I was going to die. The only thing I could do was surrender to God—give myself totally over to Him. As I did so, my fear was swallowed up by the most intense, most amazing peace I have ever known. I felt and saw myself cradled, safe and warm, in God's loving hands (just like I've seen pictures of the whole world in His hands), and nothing else mattered.[4]

I woke up still wrapped in peace, and sat up in bed, amazed. The symbolic message was clear: In one of the most perilous circumstances I could imagine, the Lord had shown me I could trust Him implicitly. I am always in His hands, always spiritually safe regardless of outward danger. We all are: "Know ye not that ye are in the hands of God? Know ye not that he hath all power?" (Mormon 5:23). That message increases in importance as calamity and evil increases in this world. That message helped me maintain my spiritual sanity when Brian died.

The Lord is so willing to bless and lift and help us. He is always there to deliver us from grief and fear and sorrow and pain. He said, "I am with you to bless you and deliver you forever" (D&C 108:8). We can count on "the great and wonderful love made manifest by the Father and the Son in the coming of the Redeemer into the world" (D&C 138:3).

Nowhere to Turn but to Christ

Sometimes I tend to run hither and yon, seeking help from all kinds of "arm of flesh" sources. I needed the reminder in Elder Richard G. Scott's talk given in the April 2008 General Conference to pull me back to the One True Source of healing. I know there is no other balm in Gilead but the Atonement of Christ and His promise to heal the broken hearted.

Elder Scott said that regardless of the source of our difficulty, and no matter how many other sources we turn to for help, that only one source offers a complete answer. Only through a broken heart and a contrite spirit, only through obedience and faith in Christ and His teachings will we find final healing.[5]

I keep going back to the Psalms for comfort and solace. One of my favorites is 55:22, "Cast thy burden upon the Lord, and he shall sustain thee." There is really nowhere else to cast it. There is no other place to turn for healing. There is no other answer. In the end we will know that the Lord's promise is real: "I have heard thy prayer, I have seen thy tears; behold, I will heal thee" (2 Kings 20:5).

Notes

1. Bruce C. Hafen, *The Broken Heart*, Deseret Book, 1998, 22.

2. See Elder Jeffrey R. Holland, "Broken Things to Mend," *Ensign*, May 2006, 71.

3. Joseph Smith, DHC vol. 5, 352.

4. Darla Isackson, *Trust God No Matter What!*, Meridian Publishing, Fairfax, Virginia, 2009, 3.

5. Richard G. Scott, "To Heal the Shattering Consequences of Abuse," *Ensign*, May 1994, 7.

The Light Returns; Life Goes On

They that sow in tears shall reap in joy.
He that goeth forth and weepeth,
bearing precious seed,
shall doubtless come again with rejoicing,
bringing his sheaves with him.

Psalm 126:5-6

16

Sunrise after Sorrow

Weeping may endure for a night,
but joy cometh in the morning.

Psalm 30:5

In the spring of 2004 I visited the ocean. I arrived late afternoon and was able to watch the sun set and a big yellow moon rise to enchant the entire seascape. The next morning I awoke just before dawn and couldn't go back to sleep. I crept quietly out of bed and stole out the back door where I could watch the sun rise over the ocean. The dark sky had begun to lighten and thin in anticipation of the dawn. The moon was still visible, but fading. Silhouettes became etched with more and more detail as the light increased. I watched in wonder as the clouds on the horizon took on an ever-increasing rosy hue.

Suddenly the top arch of the sun leapt up above the water, bright, glowing, rosy orange. The sun grew steadily to become a flaming ball that transformed the sky and sea with rays of radiant light. The rosy orange faded into a glowing border as the main body of the sun shone more and more brilliant yellow. The pink under the clouds burnt away to gray as the sun climbed higher in the sky. The glow around the sun grew increasingly bright and white; the light changed the ocean landscape from a mysterious blur to clear, crisp beauty.

I keep that sunrise filed in the archives of my memory for easy access when I need assurance that no matter how dark the night, the dawn always comes. The death of my son ushered me into a dark night of the soul, but the sun is rising again. I've learned that life tends to come in cycles; my sunshiny days don't last indefinitely; storms come, night descends, and dark clouds of trial or tragedy may obscure my view. But with every dark night there is promise of a dawn . . . because God cares and that is the way He has it set up.

All the Bad Stuff Is Temporary

Even though I'm currently living most of my days in the sunshine, I vividly remember the times I couldn't imagine rising above the clouds. At times, the struggle to keep going without seeing the sun seemed to go on and on, like it would never end. My heart felt frigid, frozen.

Storms and Cold Weather Are Temporary

One of those cold mornings I plopped myself down on the couch in the living room, hungry for inspiration, for solace, for perspective. I opened a church magazine and thumbed through it, stopping to read a story of a woman who told of her experience serving a senior mission with her husband.

She hated the cold and had been called to one of the coldest places on the planet! But she and her husband prepared well, and once there, she realized she wasn't minding the snow and storms and freezing temperatures at all. When she asked herself why, she realized it was because of the temporary nature of their stay. She realized she would have been disappointed after all their preparations if it *hadn't* been really cold.

"It Came to Pass" — Not "It Came to Stay"

The application of her story to our mortal experience was clear in my mind even before I read her take on it. No trial goes on forever! Every winter of the soul melts into spring. Our whole time here on earth is temporary! The oft-quoted scripture "And it came to pass" is literal. Nothing here in mortality comes to stay!

The struggles we have here will pass, the problems will be resolved, the tears dried. And when all is said and done, when we get to the other side, we would probably be disappointed if our mortal stay hadn't been rough and challenging—and sometimes very cold—because we prepared for it and expected it to be that way.

So why, I wondered as I put the magazine down and went back to my household chores, do I have such a hard time remembering the temporary nature of the bad stuff in life? I know in my head, but in my heart I sometimes can't comprehend that there is anything ahead but the same old struggle and sorrow and frustration—barely getting on top of dark clouds and glimpsing the sun only to find myself completely engulfed by them again.

However, her story had struck a chord. It reminded me of the scripture "My son, peace be unto thy soul; thine adversity and thine afflictions shall be but a small moment; and then if thou endure it well, God shall exalt thee on high; thou shalt triumph over all thy foes" (D&C 121:7-8).

Can we learn to *keep* the "small moment" perspective about life's hard times?

There Will Be an End to the Things We Want to End

I've heard that people resort to suicide only when their brain dysfunctions to the point that they no longer comprehend that their lives could change in positive ways. Laura Oviatt's suicide note stated she didn't believe anymore that things could get better for her. All they can see or feel is the darkness, which seems never-ending. The truth is, whether in this life or the next, light and goodness will triumph.

I lose heart only if I forget the temporary nature of the tough stuff, such as when I forget that the physical limitations I live with are not forever . . . when I forget that the frustrations of attempting to overcome

155

unhealthy childhood patterns and the constant barrage of Satan's fiery darts will someday end . . . when I forget that God will wipe away all the tears I've cried for Brian.

I sometimes fail to remember that enduring to the end means there *is* an end to the things we want to end! We are told to "hold out faithful to the end" (D&C 6:13), and, "be diligent unto the end" (D&C 10:4). That means there *is* an end to our burdens and suffering!

> *And the end shall come, and the heaven and the earth shall be consumed and pass away, and there shall be a new heaven and a new earth.*
>
> *For all old things shall pass away, and all things shall become new, even the heaven and the earth, and all the fulness thereof, both men and beasts, the fowls of the air, and the fishes of the sea. (D&C 29:23-24)*

For any of us who turn to the Lord and not away from Him, all the bad stuff *will* end—either here or hereafter. I won't struggle on the brink of depression throughout all eternity. The brain imbalances that keep me from producing sufficient "happy" chemicals are part of mortality only. I won't experience forever the frustrations of miscommunication and misunderstandings—of not seeing others as they truly are or having others miss seeing me as I truly am, of missing each others' true intent.

We understand that communication after this life is heart-to-heart, mind-to-mind. Lance Richardson tells of experiencing that kind of communication in his book *The Message.* When he was in a coma he was allowed to visit the spirit world, and said of his departed grandfather's communication:

> *I had not only heard his words with my spirit and in my mind, but I had experienced them in a most wonderful way. It seemed as if I had absorbed these words. And at the same time as the words came into my mind, I saw a picture of what he was telling me. I felt the emotions he desired to communicate to me, as well. I understood on a higher level than I ever had before.*[1]

To me that means that after this life no one can hide their truth or fail to see the truth in others. And isn't love the biggest truth we hide?

The Best News Is, the Happiest Stuff Does Not End

Of course there are many things we don't want to end—the love, the learning, the ever-growing assurance of the Lord's concern and watchful care. And they won't. Once we have triumphed through the Lord, and passed our probation—which has an end—the happy stuff endures forever. All the bad stuff in life is temporary; our sorrow over the death of our loved ones will end! 2 Nephi 8:12 says "sorrow and mourning shall flee away."

All we have to do is hang onto the Lord's promises, and remember in the dark times that the sun is there all the while, no matter how dense and dark the clouds that block our view. The thing we so often forget is that clouds are, after all, made up of life-giving water. Before long they turn into rain or snow that falls to earth and makes continued growth possible. Many of the trials in our lives, like the clouds, are full of growth-producing water in disguise.

Eternal Perspective

Charles DeFranchi, when he heard of Brian's death, e-mailed me:

> *So many Christians think of Christ in terms of his sufferings, crucifixion, and death, rather than in terms of the glorious resurrected Being He is now. [Similarly], as mortals with limited perspective, we often keep the memory of departed ones as they were when we last saw them, without realizing that many good things have happened to them since, as a result of being exposed to greater light and knowledge.*
>
> *If our paradigm is based on the memory of our departed ones as they were just before they left this world, especially if their life had not been in harmony with gospel principles, we may continue grieving until time comes for us to reunite with them. On the other hand, if we are able to consider—and especially sense through special spiritual*

experiences—that their existence has taken a new direction for the better, and that they have been transformed in the process, the grief will be replaced with the peace "that surpasseth understanding," promised by the Lord.

Remembering that, and opening my heart to the truth of Brian's life now has taken away so much of the bleakness in the landscape of my sorrow.

Winter's Branches Hold the Promise of Spring

Johann Goethe said, "Sometimes our grief resembles a fruit tree in winter. Who would think that those branches would turn green and blossom, but we hope it. We know it can happen." Perhaps the blossoming happens because we don't truly understand joy until we have experienced sorrow or love until we are faced with loss. Death and grief seem to be the ultimate teachers that give us true appreciation for what we have and can do today and motivate us to make the changes we need to make.

In her talk at Brian's funeral, my daughter-in-law, Heidi, said: "If this life were the end—the whole of our existence—then pain, failure, sorrow, and short life would indeed be a calamity. But if we look on life as eternal—stretching behind and before us—death is just a portal to the next part of our journey. Let not your hearts leave troubled today, but also do not let them leave untouched."

Sorrow Can Lead to Light

One of Deanna Edward's songs teaches us that to avoid sorrow, we'd "have to take the loving out of life." The law of opposition is a basic part of life. Joy and sorrow are flip sides of the same coin. Choosing only one side of the coin is not an option. There could be no sweet reunions without sad partings. There could be no resurrection without death. And some of my most spiritual experiences have come because of the saddest events in my life.

Because sorrow so often leads to a closer relationship with the Savior, I can count it among life's brightest sunrises. In John 16:20, 22 we read, "Ye shall be sorrowful, but your sorrow shall be turned into joy . . . And ye now therefore have sorrow: but I will see you again, and your heart shall rejoice, and your joy no man taketh from you. Jeremiah 31:13 gives us these reassuring words, "I will turn their mourning into joy, and will comfort them, and make them rejoice from their sorrow."

Every day when I turn to Him I renew my hope of the eternal sunrise of His light and love.

Notes

1. Lance Richardson, *The Message,* 2000, American Family Publications, Idaho Falls, Idaho, 55.

17

The Goal Is Progress, Not "Arriving"

O Lord, wilt thou make my path straight before me!
Wilt thou not place a stumbling block in my way—
but that thou wouldst clear my way before me,
and hedge not up my way.

2 Nephi 4:33

In spite of all the comfort, all the reassurance, sometimes it still hurts like a knife in my heart to know my son won't ever be coming through my door again in this life. Some days I still ache for Brian's physical presence. My daughter-in-law said that her worst sadness was knowing she will never see my face light up as it always did when Brian actually came to a family gathering. I have craved his presence for so many years, and didn't get nearly enough of it.

I also mourn his lost opportunities and my own lost experiences of being a part of his future achievement and happiness. I never imagined facing a future without the presence of any one of my children—I have no road map and the journey is challenging. Brian died when the leaves were blazing red and gold. I'll never hear the song "Autumn Leaves" without thinking of him. Brian is part of my heart and I long to be with him again, and to embrace him and see with my eyes that he is all right.

In short, I haven't "arrived." I'm still in the process of accepting Brian's suicide and how much that event changed the way I look at life. Some people seem to think there should be a point where we are "over" the death of our loved ones. It helps to understand that isn't the goal at all.

Jeffrey Jackson offers this thought from his handbook for those grieving a suicide: "The truth is that you will never 'get over' it, but don't let that thought discourage you. After all, what kind of people would we be if we truly got over it, as if it were something as trivial as a virus? Your hope lies in getting through it, putting your loss in its proper perspective, and accepting your life as it now lies before you, forever changed. If you can do that, the peace you seek will follow."

Brenda Floyd wrote to me saying:

I've thought repeatedly, "This year I will get better"—as if sorrow is a sickness—"this year I will grieve less." Years have absolutely nothing to do with it. Out of nowhere will come an unexpected gush of sadness and pain that cannot be touched with a finger, and I am with fresh tears again.

As for me, the tone of my questions seems to soften over the years, tears surface so much less frequently, and my awareness of life itself has deepened. Even the feeling of emptiness is softened by time and understanding.

Early on, I wrote to a friend named Janet whose son had died tragically. I knew she would understand. I said, "Brian is just so NOT HERE! The ache of missing him is so deep." She replied:

Oh dear friend, I know that ache too. It is deep, there's no getting around that. I know it took me a long time to not think of Ben all the time. But it started to register in my mind that I don't have too much longer on this planet, then Ben and I will sit and talk together. In the meantime Ben's not in pain, or in prison, and is not being abused. He's not on drugs, doesn't have any disease or any earthly malady. He's surrounded by love, by caring and kind relatives that are teaching him. He has the priesthood and Father will help him rise up to his full potential in an environment where all his wounds, spiritual and otherwise, will be healed. I think it took a while for him to get himself straight on the other side so he could accept his endowment. Now, with it, he'll have even that much more influence through the priesthood to help him get complete and right with the Lord.

Brian will have all that too. You can be sure of it. It may be too soon for you to ponder on these things. It's perfectly all right, my friend, to cry and grieve until you're through. It's okay, and it's what you should do. Talk about him all you want and write about him and dream about him and come to terms however you can. And someday it'll just dawn on you, ever so slowly, that you're starting to feel better about Brian like I do Ben. It'll come . . . I promise . . . It won't hurt this bad forever.

Love always, Janet

I echo Janet's promise, dear reader: it won't hurt this bad forever.

Starting to feel better about Brian did come. Brian is now included in the phrase in my patriarchal blessing that says I will be "inspired and influenced by loved ones who have gone before." Sometimes I do have a sense that he is inspiring and influencing me—especially with this book.

I'm grateful that Brian's name was spoken in the temple of the Lord when his temple work was completed, with his dad acting as proxy. The initiatory for men includes ordination to the office of elder in the Melchizedek Priesthood. Brian's last ordination was to the office of teacher in the Aaronic Priesthood; I feel great peace that Brian now has the opportunity for the added blessing of the Melchizedek Priesthood. I feel deep inside that he accepted it.

Progressing in Acceptance

I've stopped saying "if only." I rarely ask myself "what if?" I try to stay grounded and deal with today, with "what is." I see and feel progress. I'm not the only one. I've been heartened to talk to other suicide grievers who are even farther down the road, and to learn how well they are doing. I salute them for their courage and strength. They remind me of a quote from Robert Louis Stevenson: "Everyday courage has few witnesses. But yours is no less noble because no drum beats before you, and no crowds shout your name." I'd like to revisit some of the courageous women I've quoted in this book.

Brenda shared this healing experience:

Danny was fun-loving, and quite frankly, I've prayed that he might be allowed to be near us when the family gathers on special occasions. I know he loves and misses us. And since the night of his death, we have prayed that he is aware that we miss him and love him too. In 1992 when Danny turned eight he chose to be baptized on the 4th of July in our backyard pool. It turned out to be a very rainy day in Oregon. On another rainy July 4th in 2006, we felt Danny's presence in a particularly powerful way.

My husband, Terry, had groomed the backyard and it looked like a park. He carefully arranged ten red, white, and blue pinwheels in the shade garden around the rainbow colored spinners and sea gulls; the backyard was one large symphony of movement; everything was turning and spinning in complete harmony with the breeze. The wind chimes sang accompaniment. Shiny patriotic fringe scalloped the white plank fence and strings of clear lights dangled from the eaves of the house. Fourteen American flags fluttered on the fence line; one on each whitewashed post. He had made root-beer that is family-famous and churned his "I-just-can't-stop-myself" vanilla ice-cream! We were ready for our children and our children's children to arrive.

Indoors, I was aproned and barefoot just finishing the salads and baked beans in the polished-clean kitchen. I had opened the windows, creating a cross-breeze with energy that lifted my spirits above the kitchen's brick floor. I turned the music volume louder than usual on a Tabernacle Choir CD, and sang along as if I were in the shower. I felt like I was dancing-swirling-spinning on a cloud!

Terry rounded the corner as the song, "Homeward Bound" echoed its chorus and I burst into tears. Far out in the yard he had felt the same lifting energy and the call to come to me. We held each other as the choir cooed the tender message; "Bind me not to the pasture, chain me not to the plow, Set me free to find my calling, And I'll return to you somehow." The tears spilled over because of thoughts and feelings we had experienced separately but together, that Danny had been with us all morning long. The tender words of the song seemed to impart a powerful message to us that all was well with him—that he had work to do—and that we would be together again.

Later that day with the family gathered, the caressing breeze stiffened. Clouds my favorite color of deep storm blue rolled in and so did the children squealing from the pool. Drops of rain the size of shiny new nickels bombed the back yard. Wrapped in blankets, the patio swing held us and we could not leave the storm. It reminded us of Danny's special July 4th when it rained on his baptism. Today after five years of missing him we were all rain-soaked again with confirmed feelings that Danny was very close.

Remember April, who felt that she had disappeared within herself after her son died? Who felt that she had nothing left to give? I've been in touch with her recently and she e-mailed, "I'm doing well. I'm really in a good place after almost ten years without my son. It's a hard adjustment but I'm here. And of course every day is a reminder of him and sometimes I shed a tear or feel that it's unfair he's not here, but overall I'm okay."

My friend, Mary Smith, beautifully put into words what we all seem to be experiencing: "Grief is like the ocean—calm and peaceful, and then a wave starts to rise [higher and higher until it] breaks over one like a tsunami. The pain, the self-examination, the doubt, the tears all begin again. The wave subsides and so does the power of the grief until the next time. However, each wave gets a tiny bit smaller and the time between waves grows longer until one day you realize you have gone an hour and then two between the pain and the promise."

Bonnie is doing well. She recently wrote on her blog:

I remember the morning, in the year 2000, when I looked out my window and was startled to see snow! How could this be? Where had spring, which I love best, and early summer and golden autumn gone? And, I remember feeling astonished to realize those seasons had slipped by in that dark time of illness and grief. For several years how I could not tolerate the scent of even one single flower, when before I had loved flowers of every kind and hue! Until that month I found my house filled with gorgeous hothouse blooms wafting the cloying scent of funeral. I remember when spring came that year, how painful my beautiful season of hope and joy had become. So every year for ten years, as soon as the first crocus would begin to push out of the cold earth, I'd begin to mourn.

Eventually, I could not resist my former love. This year as the crocus peeked through the earth, I smiled it a welcome! This is the season of renewal, the season of hope, the season of the Lord's resurrection and redemption! And, the season that I have finally started to remember! To remember my firstborn baby boy—the boy I loved—the boy I still love with a mother's heart. And so I started the "Remembering Robert" blog. It's February and I'm not crying, I'm looking at his sweet baby pictures and reveling in memories—good memories! And each story and memory is bringing a smile to my face this year instead of a tear! I realize that I'm closer to my Savior than I've ever been. Hard lessons but oh, so worth it!

Brian's Gifts to Me

In retrospect, Brian gave me great gifts through both his life and his death. He taught me the meaning of the scripture in 1 Sam 16:7, "The Lord seeth not as man seeth; for man looketh on the outward appearance, but the Lord looketh on the heart." I know the Lord knows Brian's heart; he had a way of looking at other people's hearts that was not judgmental, and he had a keen aversion to hypocrisy. I was raised in a home that was judgmental, where there was a very narrow definition of acceptable behavior. I was raised in a social climate where the emphasis was placed on DOING rather than BEING, and Brian has helped squash that out of me. He taught me that it is who we ARE, not just what we DO that matters.

Brian taught me *charity*. He loved all kinds of people and they loved him back. The place where he worked closed down in order that all might come to honor his memory. Brian also taught me *compassion*. As he grew up he was tenderhearted and sensitive. When I cried he was concerned. He was aware when I was overwhelmed and I realized after he was grown that many of his needs went unmet because he was reticent to tell me, not wanting to burden me.

Because of Brian, I learned to *pray with all my heart and soul* for another human being. When he was far from the family, I sensed a little of how the Lord must feel when we will not accept His gifts and do not listen to His voice. When I read in Matthew 23:37, "How often would I have gathered thy children together, even as a hen gathereth her chickens under her wings, and ye would not!" my heart relates. After his death, I continued those prayers.

I had to learn to finally accept both the timetable of the Lord, and His utter respect for the right He gave all His children to make their own choices. If I want to be His disciple I have to have that same respect for agency.

Most of all, *I learned to say, "Thy will be done."* A scripture in D&C 101:16 became my daily source of comfort as I substituted Brian's name for the word "Zion." I would read it this way: "Let your heart be comforted concerning [Brian]; for all flesh is in mine hands; be still and know that I am God."

In those years when he was staying away from family, I experienced a mighty change of heart in regard to Brian. I changed from anger at his seeming thoughtlessness and bad choices, to an outpouring of love as the Lord led me to understand the integrity of Brian's soul. And when he left this life, I never would have guessed all I'd learn from that experience. In the years since his death I'm experiencing a mighty change of heart in regard to my whole life. I'm being transformed.

Symbolism of Spring

It has been an interesting journey as I have gone back and read the feelings I've recorded over these past few years. On April 2006 I wrote:

> *Daffodils are blooming and globe willow trees herald the coming of spring with high domes of yellow-green filigree. I've always loved spring; all through muddy March I watch with great anticipation for green sprouts to push up from buried bulbs. I also love the symbolism of dead-looking branches budding and blossoming into a glory of pink flowers and green or burgundy leaves.*
>
> *The promise of Easter is in all the newness of life I see around me. Doug came and invited me to come outside today to see sunlight shining on the frilly pink blossoms of our cherry tree. Easter has always been a special and joyful time, but it has a new and deeper meaning for me. I have scores of loved ones on the other side. All my grandmas and grandpas, aunts and uncles, my mom and dad, my brother, my son, and many friends. I long to see them again, and I know I will.*
>
> *I believe that the Easter message now has great meaning for Brian because of his new perspective of what it means to be without a body and how much he must be looking forward to having it back.*

I rejoice that a modern prophet has seen in vision those who had departed mortal life "assembled awaiting the advent of the Son of God into the spirit world, to declare their redemption from the bands of death. Their sleeping dust was to be restored unto its perfect frame, bone to his bone, and the sinews and the flesh upon them, the spirit and the body to be united never again to be divided, that they might receive a fulness of joy" (D&C 138:16-17). Each of us will have spirit and body united, never again to be divided.

I rejoice to know I will see my mother and father again! I will see Brian once more, all 6' 5" of him! I will see his brown flashing eyes and his great smile. We will embrace each other and I will know that he knows how very much I love him. The joy I will feel at that reunion I cannot begin to comprehend!

I rejoice in my testimony of the Savior, of His life and resurrection, His love and mercy, His constant invitation to come unto Him and partake of great blessings: He offers new life, new hope, new joy to all that believe on Him.

Life Goes On; New Joy Is Born

The biggest encouragement I can give you personally is that I am not only surviving, but am finding a deeper, more satisfying life. Inexplicably, I often realize lately that I'm happier than I've ever been. After I thought I had finished this book I took a couple of my granddaughters, ages three and five, to Murray Park, and suddenly I knew there was something else I wanted to say.

I haven't been to that park for years. It was the one I lived closest to when my sons were growing up. I took Brian and the other boys there so many times, and this return was full of nostalgia. The gazebo and play equipment were new, but the layout was the same, and the same great trees still spread leafy branches over the park. We walked by the river; the girls giggled and ran down a small hill and picked handfuls of dandelions, then ran onto the bridge and threw them into the river. My heart swelled with the sight of the children, so full of life, so happy. I stood on the bridge and watched the water, swift from spring runoff, carry the bright yellow baubles out of sight.

I could never have guessed the trials that lay ahead when I stood on this same bridge watching my sons throw rocks into the water thirty-some years ago. But, like the proverbial "water under the bridge" they have passed and the only thing I can change about the past is how I think about it and how I allow it to affect me. Here's the important thing: In spite of all the hard things that have happened, I am not only breathing, I am feeling joy again.

Suddenly I was struck by the message in this experience—life goes on. Every year the snow melts in the mountains and the rivers run full, and the water goes swirling and gurgling on its way. Every year the dandelions bloom, and now I'm watching a whole new generation of children pick them. The moment was precious. Every moment is.

Edwin Markham said, "Only the soul that knows the mighty grief can know the mighty rapture. Sorrows come to stretch out spaces in the heart for joy." But let me make one point absolutely clear. My joy now does *not* come from having everything just as I would like it to be.

Focusing Hope in the Right Place

About two years after Brian's death I wrote, "Much of the picture of faith in God is painted with the brush of acceptance of what is." I've changed the focus of my hope. In Moroni 7:41 we read, "And what is it that ye shall hope for? Behold, I say unto you that ye shall have hope through the Atonement of Christ and the power of his resurrection, to be raised unto life eternal, and this because of your faith in him according to the promise."

Focusing on the Savior and all His promises is my formula for peace. His love is like the light shining from the lighthouse I picked for the cover of this book. My current happiness is not based on the hope that things will "turn out" as I want, and they often don't. It is built, instead, on a deeper, firmer trust in God's reality, of Jesus' love and Atonement, of their constant concern for our welfare no matter how different life is from what I wanted or expected.

Simply put, I've finally come to peace with "what is." I've quit waging war with the parts of reality I don't like. It is true that our lives are forever changed by the suicide of someone we love, but the tragedy continues only if our changed lives are void of joy, only if we quit growing and learning and giving.

No, I haven't arrived, but step-by-baby-step, I'm coming alive in a whole new way. The Lord is good. His peace is like a river flowing through the dry land of my life. I look forward to that eternal world of joy I'll eventually inhabit, but my focus is enjoying this moment, here, today. Though I've walked a long and thorny path, I have not only survived, but the Lord is helping me live a life full of love and forgiveness. The same can be true for you!

As We End Our Journey Together...

It has meant so much to me to be able to share my journey of healing with you. I keep wishing I could sit with you, one by one, in my living room and have a personal visit . . . to give you a warm hug and share the encouragement, solace, and hope I have found. This book has been my effort to do the next best thing. As much as I've wanted to finish, I resist saying we have come to "the end." One of the most meaningful things I've learned is this: only the bad things in our lives really end!

There Will Be an End to All Sadness, Hardship, and Pain

Limitations are not forever . . . God will wipe away all the tears I've cried for Brian and there *will* be an end to the things I want to end! Hebrews 6:11 says, "And we desire that every one of you do shew the same diligence to the full assurance of hope unto the end." Matthew 13:39 adds, "The harvest is the end of the world; and the reapers are the angels."

Mortal life with all its grief will end. Heavy burdens carried here, and suffering borne, will end! All the bad stuff in life is temporary, and sorrow over the death of loved ones will end.

There Is No End to Love, Life, or Joy

Of course, I *don't want* the learning, the ever-growing assurance of the Lord's concern and watchful care, the love of family and friends to end. And they won't. In Isaiah 51:11, I found, "Therefore the redeemed of the Lord shall return, and come with singing unto Zion; and *everlasting joy* shall be upon their head: they shall obtain gladness and joy; and *sorrow and mourning shall flee away*" (emphasis added).

A New Beginning

If the good feelings start to wane, come back to this book. Review the topics you most need. Feel the love, the hope in the long-range perspective. Go to the Resource section and find scriptures there that can lift your heart and renew your spirit. Choose one of the listed Online Resources and Google it for additional help. Look at the suggested reading list and get one of those books that might enlarge your understanding. Read Debbie's story and practice some cognitive behavioral therapy to clarify your thinking. Options and sources for help abound!

All good things continue. And remember, you can always email me, so our journey together doesn't really have to end. Contact me any time at darlaisackson@gmail.com and I will respond. So let's not say good-bye. Together our hearts have been opened to the healing only God can give. We've found renewed Hope through Christ. And Hope is only the beginning!

Other Important Insights and Resources

Debbie's Story: *Includes: Controlling negative thoughts using cognitive behavioral therapy; Understanding the mindset of those contemplating suicide.*

References to Resources, Websites, Books, and Articles
Books are categorized under the following topics: suicide, grief and death, the Atonement, mental illness, addiction, suffering, forgiving, near-death experiences, pre-mortal existence, agency and our children's choices.

Life-Preserving Gift of the Scriptures
An introduction followed by a list of comforting scriptures.

Debbie's Story

Introduction by Darla Isackson

Only after I read Debbie Bake's story did I really understand how a person could actually come to the point where they felt suicide was their only option. Consequently, I'm including it here. I suggest you refer back to Debbie's graph on page 43 that shows the Contributing Factors of Major Depression. As you read her story, think about how many of those factors impacted Debbie—and your loved one as well. Debbie's explanations of cognitive therapy can help us all through the grieving process, and her insights on medication are the most enlightening I've come across.

Since her recovery, Debbie has worked professionally in a hospital setting with hundreds of people who have tried to take their own lives, which makes her story even more meaningful. She also served as a volunteer for The National Alliance on Mental Illness, which provided the opportunity to share her story and expertise with church groups, as well as support groups for those dealing with grief from a loved one's suicide. She said, "People seemed to appreciate my knowledge as a Behavioral Health Specialist; however, hearts weren't touched on an emotional level until I shared my own story of unrelenting, debilitating depression. Only then did they understand the hopelessness felt by those who are suicidal."

I know you will benefit from her story and what she has learned.

Understanding the Mindset of Those Suffering from Severe Depression

by Debbie Bake

Perhaps there were those who envied my life at one time. I was an optimistic, fun-loving and spiritual woman who adored her husband. I loved life and had idealistic goals which I had every reason to believe would be fulfilled. My aspirations were falling neatly into place when I learned I was pregnant during my final semester in college. Little did I know that it would have been easier to predict the date and place of the next earthquake than guess my life's course over the next thirteen years.

In the beginning, from my outward appearance, few people knew I struggled with depression—not even me. I complained to doctors about headaches, stomach problems, stress, and fatigue. My obvious physical symptoms allowed the real problem (the turmoil raging in my mind) to go undetected.

After a difficult pregnancy our twin girls (each weighing 5.2 pounds) were born on June 18, 1977. My joy soon gave way to sorrow as I learned one baby did not survive. To comfort me, some offered their support by saying such things as, "Just be grateful you still have a baby"—as if the baby lost didn't matter. This gave way to silent grief that was compounded by the fear we would also lose our surviving twin.

These fears seemed groundless when we observed how well our baby nursed and slept. But then, six weeks later, an abrupt change occurred: our baby began to cry relentlessly. I could only assume her discomfort was somehow my fault and commenced to rehearse in my mind all the reasons I was no longer competent as a person or a mother.

Frequent trips to the doctor and numerous painful tests provided no answers, and not being able to help one so helpless left me in a state of grief such as I had never felt before. Then overwhelming anxiety took hold, intensifying with each new health problem that emerged in our baby daughter. I often wondered how my husband was able to sleep during unbelievable bouts of crying—not only from the baby but myself.

Nine months later we learned the reason for our daughter's distress: she had a kidney disease that had been undetected. Her suffering was not caused by my lack after all. Somehow though, I never challenged or erased my negative conclusions about myself and they became a magnet for subsequent distressing thoughts.

Then a succession of other traumatic events ensued, each leaving piranha-type lacerations in my heart and mind—allowing self-confidence, spirituality, and previous security to slowly ebb away. Thus, I began to experience nothing except fear-based thoughts and gripping awareness of perceived impending doom. Many well-meaning people suggested that Satan was the cause of such thoughts, so I embarked on a plan to increase my spirituality by doubling my efforts in scripture study, prayer, temple attendance, and service to others. These efforts only left me exhausted and even more distraught than before.

Sundays had always been my favorite day of the week, but soon became void of pleasure. I dreaded even the thought of going to church where I felt the necessity of exhibiting a pasted-on smile. The energy to maintain such a facade drained my strength, as did the inevitable greetings of others. Just a simple phrase, "How are you?" caused embarrassment as my mind raced through a thousand scenarios of how I really was. Each time, a simple "I'm fine" managed to escape my lips, but the incongruence of my answer left me disheartened and empty.

I had previously been sensitive to the tutelage, inspiration, and peace received from closeness to God; consequently, not feeling the Spirit was unbearable. I couldn't reconcile in my mind why I was unable to lift myself in order to enjoy promised blessings of peace offered to those who keep the Lord's commandments. I felt as if the love of God had been stripped away from me, leaving behind a terrified victim—naked and vulnerable.

I wish I could have understood that the true source of my emotional distress was an illness, not unworthiness or the harsh buffetings of Satan reserved for those who knowingly sin and remain unrepentant. Instead, I believe my unbridled negative thoughts gained momentum as a result of sleep deprivation, high stress, ineffective coping skills, and other factors which eventually led to more physical and mental dysfunction.

Diagnosis

About five years after the birth of our twins I was finally diagnosed with clinical depression. I was thrilled to learn that what I was experiencing had a name and that it was treatable. After educating myself about depression, I religiously worked on a personal recovery plan which included various antidepressant medications, counseling, support groups, self-help books, priesthood blessings, Know Your Religion and Institute classes, exercise, and a vegetarian diet. When these methods failed to give the desired results, I engaged in alternative medicine treatments—all of which were costly and ineffective at treating my severe depression.

It is impossible to express how difficult it was to make myself do the above tasks, and the overwhelming discouragement after such massive physical and emotional effort. Most of the time I stayed in bed, but sometimes I forced my-self to get up to try one more suggested avenue of relief. I followed this pattern over and over again, month after month, then year after year.

After nine years of unrelenting depression and suicidal ideation, I learned that I was pregnant. Even though I yearned for more children, my husband and I wondered how I could care for a baby when I already struggled to care for our daughter. I was promised, through a priesthood blessing, that the Lord was answering our prayers, and that our baby's birth would bring new life and healing to us all.

When I was five months along we were shocked when labor pains threatened to end our promised miracle. We rushed to the hospital and I was examined by a doctor who assured me that I had a good chance of keeping the baby, but the pains continued to intensify. As my husband, Drew, leaned over my hospital bed he tenderly held my hand, and then instinctively fell to his knees and through tears of deep emotion prayed out loud for me. (He showed no hesitation even though others were in the room.)

My husband asked the Lord to stop my labor pains and humbly explained how much we wanted to keep our baby. He then added, "If it is not thy will and our baby won't survive, please let him come quickly so Deb won't have to stay in such pain." He pledged that we would trust Him and His will no matter the outcome. Within a few minutes our son was born . . . only to leave mortality as quickly as he had been delivered.

Desiring to stay true to our covenant with Heavenly Father, we did not complain or feel anger at the seeming injustice of it all. And upon the Lord's witness of our faith He blessed us with a marvelous experience that we treasure to this day. (Trusting God through this experience was the exact opposite of the fear which blocked emotional comfort when our twin daughter died.)

Our dear bishop blessed me, saying that the Lord would still allow me to raise a son and would soon provide His promised healing. With this encouragement, we proceeded with adoption plans. Shortly thereafter we welcomed a precious baby boy into our home, but not the expected healing of my depression. We asked the Lord to speed my recovery for the sake of our children, but for reasons beyond our comprehension my illness heightened and began to micro-manage my mind, body, and spirit. As a result, my world as I knew it ceased to exist.

Before our son turned a year old I was no longer able to function. Inconceivably, I not only found myself with the same precarious instability, but I also experienced an increase in the intensity of suicidal thoughts. As a last resort, I decided to try electroconvulsive therapy (ECT). It was reported to benefit others who were severely depressed (sometimes after only a few treatments), and this new hope permeated our home. My sister, who had four young boys of her own, graciously cared for my children during my hospital stay, and extended family prayed that ECT would be the avenue for some measure of relief. I received a series of twelve bilateral treatments over a four-week period, but they provided no benefit.

Meanwhile, I continued to seek priesthood blessings, many of which also promised healing. I was certain the Lord would work His mighty miracle each time I was blessed (and I did improve for a day or two), but no matter how hard I tried to stay positive, I continued to be distressed and unable to cope with life.

Friends and family wondered why I couldn't just lift myself out of depression by thinking positive thoughts. I wondered too. I came from a family that maintained a positive outlook on life in spite of many health challenges; I had learned to do the same. But this was different: no matter how hard I tried I could not conjure up one happy thought.

It didn't help matters when I heard the phrase, "No unhappy person will inherit the celestial kingdom" (spoken at a BYU fireside). It felt like a personal chastisement for my inability to cope. (And with my thinking ability impaired, I could not evaluate the true meaning behind this statement.) So I created one more thought distortion to add to an ever-increasing list of self-incriminating thoughts—believing that my heavenly inheritance was no longer within my reach.

Soon I was unable to get out of bed. I feared everything; I found pleasure in nothing. All I could do was sob out my lamentations to those who had heard them hundreds of times before. I was told over and over again that things would get better, to just hang on . . . but after years of continued suicidal ideation, the encouragement of others began to fall on deaf ears and a numb heart.

As my illness progressed to its most severe point I became unable to cry or speak. Family would call only to reach the answering machine. They begged me to pick up the phone but I turned my face to the wall in shame. I rarely communicated with anyone and felt as if I was already dead, trapped in a body and brain that refused to die. Meanwhile, each minute seemed to last for hours, with days and nights that had no distinction from each other. My only relief came when I was asleep.

My dear husband was at a loss. He had taken on the extra roles of mom, house cleaner, meal preparer, and safety inspector. He was so kind, and yet I didn't comprehend how much he loved me, and that his sincere desire was to care for me and our children as long as necessary. He begged me to not harm myself but I had other plans. I had been suicidal for years; now, however, I contrived a specific plan of how I could end the pain for myself and quit being a burden on those who cared about me most. Understandably, I earned the right to another trip—with the psychiatric unit as the explicit destination.

After six weeks of hospitalization, the only result was overwhelming guilt that riddled my mind from not fulfilling my responsibilities as a mother. I questioned how much my illness would affect our children in later years, and became convinced that my continued survival would mean their inevitable downfall.

When faced with such a dichotomy between promised healing and the actual outcome, I searched for reasons that might explain the unexplainable. I concluded that the Lord had given up on me because I was unable to do what any good wife, mother, and believer in Christ should be doing. I used all the good things I'd learned in church to whip myself, and I mourned the loss of the person I once was. I remember crying out (perhaps "screaming" would be more accurate) to the Lord, "Why didn't you take me home when I was still a good person!—just look at me now."

Thought Distortions

I had been reduced to a shell of a person lingering between life and death with persistent, negative thoughts which held me hostage twenty-four hours a day. Heaven knows people tried, but no one could convince me that the following thoughts were not grounded in reality:

- I am a horrible mother. My children would be better off if I were dead.
- My husband deserves a wife that is normal. He won't divorce me, so I need to die so that he can be blessed with a better spouse.
- No one understands the depth of emotional pain I am feeling and how hard I've tried to overcome this illness. I am a failure.
- I am worthless and a waste of space on this planet.

- God is disappointed with my inability to cope.
- I'll never be able to feel the Spirit again. My faith is weak. Satan has power over me now. There is no hope of getting better.
- My death will free others from the pain I am causing them.
- Suicide is the only option left.

Is it so unfathomable to imagine that someone can no longer go on living in such a condition? All colors in my world had turned to gray.

Perfect in Christ

I had an experience that would forever change my way of thinking concerning my self-worth and value to God. It took place on a day like all the others had been. I remember struggling to get out of bed to use the bathroom. After washing my hands I accidentally broke my cardinal rule to not look up into our mirror over the sink and found myself staring into the face of someone who slightly resembled me. I said with complete conviction, "You are the most ugly, pathetic creature God ever created!"

Imagine my surprise when I heard the following words spoken clearly to my mind, "Debbie, you are perfect in your own sphere." I wasn't sure what the word "sphere" meant. When my husband came home from work I related this experience to him. He smiled and explained that the word sphere probably referred to my realm or situation. My sphere was depression and even though I couldn't fulfill any of my responsibilities, the Lord found me acceptable and perfect through Christ. This realization jolted me out of my most negative thoughts about myself and gave me a measure of comfort.

I share the above story to give those suffering from a feeling of low self-worth (for any reason) a stronger hope in Christ, and His tender love and acceptance of us when we simply do the best we can. I now realize that my illness is what kept me from *feeling* the spiritual help that was there for me all along.

Even after such a powerful witness as to my worth, I continued to decline.

Several years passed, each seemingly worse than the last. I had lost not only peace of mind but also any semblance of physical health. I believed I would soon die without heavenly intervention. Peering out our window I watched as my family and neighbors celebrated the New Year, barely having the strength to stand; yet, I found myself engrossed in mighty prayer.

I heard myself crying out, "Heavenly Father, please have compassion on me!" I then promised to trust Him even if healing never came. Somehow, I could feel my faith being renewed as I prayed, so I continued. I told the Lord that I could survive and cope with a depressed mood, but not the constant barrage of enticements to take my own life. I sincerely thanked Him for a loving husband who was an anchor for our family, and asked for patience to endure my trial until release came, in whatever form that might take. And I asked once again (even though this had been my plea ever since the birth of our twins) that He take all suicidal thoughts from me.

A New Beginning

At that very moment—even before I closed my prayer—just minutes after midnight on January 1, 1990, my reprieve was granted. Through the grace of God I was healed from the intense, haunting suicidal thoughts that had plagued me for thirteen years.

When I told my husband about the removal of these thoughts, he looked at me with more compassion than I had ever seen in his face before. He said, "Oh, Debbie, please don't be upset if you become suicidal once again." He had watched me gain hope after priesthood blessings, being sure this was the blessing that would end my exquisite pain, only to have hopelessness return soon afterward. But I knew this time was different. I could literally feel a change in my brain.

I don't know how the Lord was able to take away my suicidal thoughts while leaving behind depression for me to manage; I only know that He did. And to this day (twenty years later) I continue to give honor and praise to God for this miracle. My nightmare ended, allowing me to eventually see life in living color once again.

In 1990 I learned that undiagnosed hormonal problems and fibromyalgia also contributed to my mental and physical pain. And though depression continues to be a thorn in my side, I am able to control it through a combination of medications and learning new coping skills—such as stress management, assertiveness training, acceptance of factors beyond my control, faith, and challenging my false beliefs through cognitive behavioral therapy—CBT.

CBT is one technique that has had a positive impact in my recovery, and continues to be a blessing in my life. For this reason, Darla has asked me to explain it.

Cognitive Behavioral Therapy

Medication may offer stability, but it is not the only thing that changes brain chemistry. Research has shown cognitive behavioral therapy to be as effective as any other form of treatment for depression (except, perhaps, for severe cases where the need for psychotropic drugs in combination with CBT may be warranted). And, has proven (more than medication) to decrease the likelihood of relapse.

Cognitive behavioral therapy is a combination of behavior therapy and cognitive therapy. It is based on the idea that changing the way we think allows us to feel better and act better even if one's situation doesn't change. Those who develop irrational beliefs in childhood may never challenge these destructive thought patterns even in adulthood. As a result, these automatic negative thoughts take on a life of their own.

I've come to recognize that the foundation blocks of depression are built on lies, and the truth about our spiritual identity—our basic spirit self—is lost in the mire of unchecked thought distortions. In order to disrupt thinking errors, one must learn how to challenge uninvited, damaging thoughts.

A psychiatrist gave me an assignment to write three of my most dominant, negative thoughts, and then to list three reasons why each of these thoughts *may not* be true. (When I tried to tell myself the negative thought was NOT true, my brain would cling even harder to that negative belief.) Such a simple assignment, yet it took an entire week to even think of three reasons why I wasn't a "horrible" mother. But once the assignment was completed I was able to unlock my fixated thought and replace it with a kinder, more insightful belief.

Here's an example of how I reframed one of my unwanted negative thoughts.

Negative thought: I am a horrible mother.

Reframe your thought to make it more accurate: (What else could be true?)

1. *I love my children.*
2. *I give them hugs.*
3. *I do the best I can.*

Using this simple technique allowed me to find relief from false ideas that kept me stuck in despair. I could then channel the emotional energy I had previously employed to shame myself into more constructive venues.

I wrote each thought distortion on a separate 3x5 card and kept these cards in my pocket so I could read them out loud whenever a particular negative thought surfaced. (Of course I found that I needed more than three, 3x5 cards!)

How CBT Can Help You

We are all at risk for self-incriminating thoughts that can rob us of peace. Whether they come from Satan, from the illness itself, or from the negative tendencies of the natural man mind, the brain is bombarded with the kind of self-loathing I expressed when I looked in the mirror. Challenging our negative beliefs is one of the best ways I know of for protecting us against the lies that spread their infectious venom throughout our mind, spirit, and body.

Even children can learn how to challenge their negative thoughts if they are provided with incentives. Doing so would give them an early start with practicing good mental health. Then, instead of being frustrated as I was when told to "just think positive," they would actually have a tool to help them achieve this goal.

I wish every person could read the book *Feeling Good: The New Mood Therapy,* written by an innovative and popular psychiatrist, David Burns.[1] His book brings cognitive therapy to the forefront and made a profound difference in my ability to challenge my thoughts. He also has a companion book entitled, *The Feeling Good Handbook,*[2] which provides exercises to help readers overcome negative thinking patterns. There are also weekly self-assessment tests to monitor progress as the reader applies the principles in the workbook.

But let us remember that God is the Master over CBT. We would do well to follow His guidance as put forth in the Book of Mormon:

> *But this much I can tell you, that if ye do not watch yourselves, and your thoughts, and your words, and your deeds, and observe the commandments of God, and continue in faith of what ye have heard concerning the coming of our Lord, even unto the end of your lives, ye must perish. And now, O man, remember, and perish not." (Mosiah 4:30)*

Conversely, here is my modern-day equivalent of the above verse:

If we watch ourselves—hoping and believing faith-based thoughts, these thoughts will give way to positive feelings and words, which in turn will influence our behavior for good, whereby we will desire to keep God's commandments and generate even more faith to endure trials, and in the end we will be exalted to enjoy the lasting fruits of Godly peace and joy for ever more. And now, O dearest brothers and sisters, remember these sayings and live (Debbie 28:1).

What about Antidepressants?

I appreciate and value many of the characteristics passed down to me through my ancestry, except, of course, the genetic predisposition for depression. My friend, Dr. Russ Seigenberg, states, "Some people have a genetic predisposition to depression and may be more sensitive (and less adaptable) to stress than others. These individuals are more likely to require medication."

After years of being homebound and brain-bound, I was excited to learn that CBT could speed my recovery; however, I lacked the mental clarity and was too fatigued to do cognitive work. After trying countless antidepressants, imagine how grateful I was when a skilled psychiatrist tried a combination of two medications that were not only tolerable but also effective for me. Only then did I have the energy and capacity to concentrate and fully implement the techniques of cognitive behavioral therapy. Medication can truly be a Godsend (when used properly and when combined with CBT).

On the other hand, as much as I appreciate the benefits of medication, I still believe there has been an over-emphasis on drug therapy, especially in light of scientific evidence that things other than drugs can *change* brain chemistry. It is vital to understand that *medication alone can never take the place of the hard work involved in overcoming multiplex factors which keep the brain at risk for addictions and mood disorders.* For this reason I think it is important to understand the limitations of antidepressants.

Medication alone can never resolve one's psychological problems of worrying, self-criticism, pain of losing a loved one, irrational thoughts (such a guilt and hopelessness); situational issues such as financial or relationship problems, or limited coping ability; spiritual deficits, which may include being blinded to the love of God even when that love is shown through His earthly angels; or biological factors that may continue to influence mood in spite of an antidepressant. (See chart in chapter four for more details.)

Due to the unpleasant and sometimes dangerous side effects of medications (such as headaches, lack of emotion, constipation, seizures, sexual dysfunction, anxiety, sometimes even depression and suicidal ideation), we would be better served by *first* looking for solutions to factors (such as those listed above) that may be contributing to our problems.

Caring for Those Who Suffer

In my mind, it is simply unconscionable that many who suffer from emotional or mental illness do not have the benefit of counseling or medications. And those that do have access may still struggle beyond imagination. For this reason, I promised Heavenly Father that if I overcame suicidal thoughts I would spend the rest of my life trying to bless those who suffer.

My first opportunity to serve came in the form of a job at an area hospital where I had the opportunity to teach coping skills and cognitive behavioral therapy to depressed patients, many of whom had attempted suicide. After ten years of hearing their stories, I'd like to share some of their thoughts (along with my own) concerning the mindset of suicidal persons.

Mindset of Those Contemplating Suicide

No single event caused your loved one to give up. There are always multiple factors that contribute to depression. What you did or did not do is not the reason for their attempt or completion of suicide. Biological, psychological and environmental (or situational) factors may converge, leading some to believe they have no hope of recovery. (See chart on page 43 showing the multiple factors involved.)

Your loved one was only thinking of their own pain, not the pain they would cause countless others. Many patients expressed sadness at learning how their suicide attempt affected their families. The goal wasn't to die: it was simply a resolution to rid themselves of unbearable suffering. Some even reported that their attempt was meant to be a scream for help and were upset to learn they almost died.

Many believed that suicide would bring relief to their caregivers. Sometimes it doesn't matter how much you tell or show someone they aren't a burden; they hold so tightly to that thought distortion, they can no longer see the truth.

Most coped the best way they knew how. Addiction to alcohol or street drugs is often a result of self-medicating. Some may become workaholics, watch mindless television, or use round- the-clock sleeping to numb themselves. Regardless of one's ineffective coping mechanisms, the primary reason these negative behaviors continue is because of the inability to rid oneself of emotional turmoil. (I had never considered using drugs or alcohol until my depression was at its worst. If these substances had been readily available to me, I have no doubt that I would have used them. I now have great empathy for those suffering from addictions and realize that many may not even know they are self-medicating due to symptoms of an underlying mental illness.)

They did not give up without a valiant fight. Perhaps you know individuals who suffer horrific physical pain and wonder why they are able to withstand life's fiery darts while your cherished family member gave up without so much as consulting you. But, we can never understand the severity of depression in others unless we have experienced it with the same intensity and duration— maybe not even then.

Imagine having a mental illness, poor coping skills, perhaps an addiction to drugs or alcohol, and no personal hope for recovery. That is the mindset of many who contemplate suicide.

It is hard for me to admit, but I think you should know: my survival during those years of relentless suicidal ideation had nothing to do with being any more spiritual or stronger than those that die by suicide—*if I had had the energy to get out of bed and leave the house to carry out a plan, I probably would not be here today.* I don't understand why some recover while others do not; I only know that trusting the Lord's wisdom, even in the face of un-answered questions, will bring us closer to the ultimate joy our Savior gave up His life to share.

Conclusion

I often watch awards being given out for various accomplishments in life deemed to be extraordinary, such as the academy awards, gold medals from the Olympics, sports trophies from celebrated athletes. I think there ought to be a new award just for those that swim in mental illness, where the pool is filled with quicksand instead of water. Your loved one who died most assuredly deserves many gold medals for all the times they put forth a Herculean effort to survive just one more day.

Do you remember when I said that all my doubled efforts to increase spirituality caused my depression to worsen? I cannot conclude without reminding you (and myself) that the Lord never asks us to run faster than we have strength. I often depleted my physical and spiritual reserves, as I tried to "run" in spite of an empty reservoir. But I did the best I could with the knowledge I had at the time. That is all that God requires.

Take heart. Our Creator is in charge. He knows the true spirit of your loved one, and has given them (and each of us) all eternity to continue growing into their potential.

Notes

1. David D. Burns, *The New Mood Therapy,* 1980; Avon Books, an imprint of HarperCollins Publishers; revised and updated, 1981.

2. David D. Burns, *The Feeling Good Handbook,* 1990; revised edition, 1999 HarperCollins Publishers.

Websites

American Foundation for Suicide Prevention
Go to www.AFSP.org then click on "About Suicide" and "Find Support," which should give you the option to talk with someone who has also lost someone to suicide.

Grief Support Center
Includes an index of grief support centers and hotlines, one-on-one grief counseling, education concerning suicide (such as a list of ten characteristics most commonly associated with completed suicide). Google www.belovedhearts.com then click on "Grief Support Center at Beloved Hearts."

S.O.S. (Survivors of Suicide)
When you Google "SOS support groups" you will find several reputable national organizations. One of them might be near you.

Willowgreen
James E. Miller has an excellent website. After you go to www.willowgreen.com click on "Grief Advice" for uplifting information in several categories such as "When You're First Grieving," and "When Crisis Has Changed Your Life." For the text I quoted from in this book, click on "When You Feel Sad." On this site you will also have the option to order excellent books, videotapes and audio tapes in the areas of loss, grief, illness, and dying, etc., such as *Listen to Your Sadness: Finding Hope Again after Despair Invades Your Life.*

Grief Watch
The website www.griefwatch.com offers bereavement resources, memorial products and links that can help you through your personal loss.

Centering Corporation—Your Grief Resource Center
The Grief Resource Center is a family owned and operated business (similar to Grief Watch) that is dedicated to serving the needs of those healing from loss.

Centering Corporation offers one of the largest mail order and online selections of bereavement titles available. www.centering.org

Doug Manning's Care Community and In-sight Books
Doug Manning is one of the best-loved authors and speakers in the areas of grief and elder care. Go to www.TheCareCommunity.com to read Doug's blogs on grief. Click "Beginning the Journey" to check out Doug's permanent blog for those who are fresh in their grief. Google Doug's "In-sight Books" for a large listing of grief support resources, available to you in the quickest and most organized way possible.

Webhealing
The Internet's first interactive grief website, serving the bereaved on the net since 1995. It offers grief discussion boards where men and women can discuss issues related to grief and healing, or browse recommended grief books. www.Webhealing.com

The Compassionate Friends
The mission of The Compassionate Friends is to assist families toward the positive resolution of grief following the death of a child of any age, and to provide information to help others be supportive. Site includes a chapter locater for finding a group in your own city. www.compassionatefriends.org

Suicide Prevention Action Network
Excellent suicide prevention websites with resources for suicide grievers (who are often referred to as "survivors"). www.spanusa.org

Emotional Freedom Technique
Grievers often find emotional clearing helpful. Find online the emotional freedom technique (EFT) for emotional clearing. Google "EFT" and receive instruction to try the Emotional Freedom Technique independently, or contact one of the many skilled therapists who us EFT.

The International Association for Near-Death Studies (IANDS)
IANDS is an educational nonprofit 501(c)(3) organization, which focuses most of its resources into providing the highest quality information available about Near-Death Experiences. They publish a peer-reviewed scholarly journal and

a member newsletter, and sponsor conferences and other programs. See www. iands.org for more information.

IANDS offers a Free Downloadable Eleven-Page Research Paper—by the lead researcher, a Cardiologist of the largest hospital-based NDE study—about the implications of near-death experiences. Van Lommel, Pim, "*About the Continuity of Our Consciousness*," The International Association for Near-Death Studies, 18 Aug 2005. <http://iands.org/research/vanLommel/vanLommel.php>

Utah-based Support Groups

Caring Connections: A program of the National Hospice and Palliative Care Organization (NHPCO).

Caring Connections: A Hope and Comfort in Grief is a non-profit bereavement care program located with the University of Utah College of Nursing, and is directed by Katherine P. *Supiano, PhD, LCSW, FT.*

The Mission of Caring Connections is: To provide excellent evidence-based bereavement care to grieving persons in the intermountain west through clinician facilitated support groups; and, in keeping with the academic mission of the University and the College of Nursing, to provide opportunity for clinical education in grief and loss to students in the health care professions, and to conduct research which promotes greater understanding of loss, grief and bereavement.

They offer 8-week clinician-facilitated grief support groups for survivors of suicide three times yearly in three locations. For information or to register, please call 801-585-9522 or visit our website http://nursing.utah.edu/caring-connections/index.php

The Sharing Place: A grief support program for children in the Salt Lake area.
1695 East 3300 South
Salt Lake City, UT 84106
Phone: 801-466-6730

General Market Books on Suicide and Grief

A Handbook for Survivors of Suicide
Jeffrey Jackson, Published by the American Association of Suicidology.
The author is a survivor of an attempted suicide himself and his book is one of the best general guides I've found. It is free and easy to access on the internet. Just Google A Handbook for Survivors of Suicide and it will come up. (This book is one of the resources I was given at the Caring Connections support group. I was madly marking information that I wanted to share before I discovered that you could easily download a PDF file of this excellent thirty-six page booklet for free. I suggest you get this handbook and study it. The wording is so clear and the explanations feel so right.)

Suicide Survivors—A Guide for Those Left Behind
Adina Wrobleski, Published by Afterwords, 1994.
Helpful and insightful information for suicide survivors; it is honest, open, and easy to read. The website says: "It may be one of the best, most accurate books ever published on suicide/suicide grief. Adina Wrobleski is an expert on suicide, having spent many years studying the subject after her daughter died by suicide. Reading this book might be a good 'first step' for someone beginning the arduous journey of trying to work through suicide grief." (Adina Wrobleski has also written an excellent booklet called Suicide Why: 85 Questions and Answers about Suicide.)

My Son . . . My Son: A Guide to Healing After Death, Loss, or Suicide
Iris Bolton, Bolton Press, Atlanta, GA, 1983.
I remember this book being especially helpful to me a few months after Brian's death. Written by a mother who knows what it's like, it is filled with compassion and sound advice.

The Grief Recovery Handbook: The Action Program for Moving beyond Death, Divorce, and Other Losses
John W. James and Russell Friedman, Harper Perennial, revised edition, 1998.
This book gives excellent and practical grief-work help and understanding, including exercises to help us work through unfinished business and give undelivered messages to those we have lost.

Why Suicide
Eric Marcus Harper, San Francisco, CA, 1996.
Includes helpful information on topics such as these: what to say and not to say to survivors, how to help grieving children, how to cope with the suicide of someone you know, suicide and the elderly (teen/youth), treatment and prevention.

A Sacred Sorrow: Reaching Out to God in the Lost Language of Lament
Michael Card, NavPress, Colorado Springs, CO, 2005.
A Christian book with an important message. Back cover text states, "It's easy to praise God when things in your life are going well, but what about the other times? What happens when mountaintop experiences cascade into seasons of struggling in the valley? God desires for us to pour out our hearts to Him, whether in joy or pain. But many of us don't feel right expressing our anger, frustrations, and sadness in prayer. Our personal worship experience is not complete unless we understand the lost language of lament."

Books Written for the LDS Audience

Author's note: Most of the books listed are now available in e-book formats as well as print. Many are also available as audio books. Google the publisher or Amazon.com for more information.

Suicide specific

Suicide: Some Things We Know, and Some We Do Not
M. Russell Ballard, Deseret Book Company, Salt Lake City, UT, 1993.
The most "official" information we have on the Church's stand on the subject. Written by a General Authority, this little booklet relieved many of my fears and helped me sort through the doctrinal implications of Brian's death by suicide.

Where Is Our Hope for Peace?
Jaynann M. Payne & Dr. Rick, Hidden Treasures Institute, Ogden, UT, 2001.
This is a helpful and comforting book. Brenda Floyd said, "This is the book you must read even if you read nothing else. It was probably the most valuable book I read. Ironically it was published the year I lost my son."

Grief and death

What's on the Other Side? – What the Gospel Teaches Us about the Spirit World
Brent L. Top, Deseret Book, Salt Lake City, UT, 2012
The Prophet Joseph Smith observed that death and the spirit world are subjects that we ought to study more than any other. Here we find a wealth of information from scriptures and latter-day prophets and apostles about death and the spirit world, its location and conditions, the nature of departed spirits, and the work performed by those there.

Grieving: The Pain and the Promise
Deanna Edwards, Covenant Communications, Inc., American Fork, UT, 1989.
Deanna's book has become a classic for giving support through the grief process. It also offers a vision of the spiritual gifts grief can offer and the opportunity to create because of it.

Jesus Wept
Joyce & Dennis Ashton, Bonneville Books, Cedar Fort, Inc., Springville, UT, 2001.
A collection of stories and gospel perspective for understanding and enduring loss of all kinds (including suicide), as part of the process of enduring to the end. Joyce and Dennis Ashton also wrote *Loss and Grief Recovery*, which addresses the many faces of adversity and why bad things happen to good people.

The Gateway We Call Death
Russell M. Nelson, Deseret Book Company, Salt Lake City, UT, 1995.
Some of the topics discussed in this book: the purpose of life, the purpose of mourning, when death comes without warning, factors of choice, and life after death.

Mourning with Those Who Mourn
Steven C. Walker & Jane D. Brady, Bookcraft, Inc., Salt Lake City, UT, 1999.
Latter-day Saints share experiences and perspectives on loss and grieving in an articulate and inspiring manner. They share sensitive emotions concerning a wide range of losses. This book is meant to add hope as well as insight and comfort and give the assurance that you are not alone.

Beyond Death's Door
Brent L. Top & Wendy C. Top, Bookcraft, Inc., Salt Lake City, UT, 1993.
Comparing near-death accounts and the doctrines of the restored gospel of

Jesus Christ, offering comfort and interesting insights into death and the spirit world.

Life after Death

Robert L. Millett, Deseret Book Company, Salt Lake City, UT, 1999.

From the dust jacket of this book we read, "Strictly speaking, there is no death and there are no dead. When things die they do not cease to be; they merely cease to be in this world. Life goes on. Death is a transition."

Joy, The Other Side of Sorrow

Steven Dunn Hanson, Bookcraft, Inc., Salt Lake City, UT, 1992.

This book can be read for free on Kindle Unlimited or purchased for a low price on Amazon.com. In the introduction of this book we read, "To see and to experience the paradox of the joy which comes from sorrow is to know something of Christ." Steven Hanson's book is based on a "wide range of interviews with people who have experienced this paradox."

The Atonement

The Infinite Atonement

Tad R. Callister, Deseret Book Company, Salt Lake City, UT, 2000.

An amazing, uplifting, informative book on the Atonement of Christ. Answers some of life's deepest and most important questions.

Believing Christ

Stephen E. Robinson, Deseret Book Company, Salt Lake City, UT, 1992.

Chapter titles: The Great Dilemma, Good News, The Covenant, Saved by Grace, Misunderstanding Grace, and "Lord, How Is It Done?" Brother Robinson explains the Savior's Atonement through vivid analogies, stories, and plainspoken words. The Good News of the gospel presented in an incredibly understandable way.

The Broken Heart: Applying the Atonement to Life's Experiences

Bruce C. Hafen, Deseret Book Company, Salt Lake City, UT, 1998. (A new expanded edition in paperback was released in 2008.)

An excellent book that clearly explains the breath-taking width and breadth of the Atonement's application to our lives. Easy reading, straightforward, comforting.

In the Arms of His Love
Steven Cramer, Covenant Communications, American Fork, UT, 1991. (New soft cover edition, 2010.)
Steven Cramer gives an amazingly clear profile of the Savior's love and suggests nine steps we can take to grow closer to the Lord. Using scriptural documentation and personal testimony, Brother Cramer helps us experience the profound and unconditional love of the Savior and the significance of His Atonement. Helps restore hope and gives renewed strength and joy as we feel encircled in the loving arms of the Savior.

Mental Illness

Valley of Sorrow: A Layman's Guide to Understanding Mental Illness
Alexander B. Morrison, Deseret Book Company, Salt Lake City, UT, 2003.
Writing from the perspective of a father with a close family member who has for many years been afflicted with a chronic mental illness that no treatment has alleviated. Elder Morrison, an emeritus General Authority, offers understanding and hope and valuable perspectives on mental illness, suffering, and suicide.

Addiction

Understanding Alcohol and Drug Addiction: An LDS Perspective
Merlin O. Baker, Cedar Fort Publishing, Springville, UT, 2004.

Suffering in general

Making Sense of Suffering
Wayne E. Brickey, Deseret Book Company, Salt Lake City, UT, 2001.
Brickey takes your hand and tenderly teaches the precious elements of the refiner's fire. Not only will you come to understand the purpose in suffering, but you shall also come to trust and love that One who suffered for all.

All These Things Shall Give Thee Experience
Neal A. Maxwell, Deseret Book Company, Salt Lake City, UT, 1979.
As Elder Maxwell states: "to be untested and unproven is also to be unaware of all that we are . . . even if we plead otherwise . . . He must at times say no."

Pain Is Inevitable, Misery Is Optional
Hyrum W. Smith with Gerreld L. Pulsipher, Deseret Book Company, Salt Lake City, UT, 2004. (Also available in audio format.)
Having been asked to speak (as a former mission president) at the funeral of one of his former missionaries, Hyrum W. Smith draws upon personal experiences and lessons he learned about pain, endurance, self-deception, God's Plan for our lives, and the power of the Savior's Atonement.

Trust God No Matter What!
Darla Isackson, Meridian Publishing, Fairfax, VA, 2009. Now distributed by Digital Legends and available on Amazon.com in print and ebook formats.
"Trusting God When Prayers Don't Seem Answered," "Trusting God When We Are Hurting," and "Trusting God When Children Stray" are some of the sections in this 300-page book. A reviewer said, "The Contents list alone reaches out and promises balm for some of life's hardest dilemmas, and the text delivers. In *Trust God No Matter What!* you'll find no 'same-old' worn words, but fresh, honest, comforting, enlightening Christ-centered insights."

Forgiving

Forgiveness: The Healing Gift We Give Ourselves
Cheryl Carson, Self-published, 7th printing (revised and expanded), 1998.
If forgiving others is an issue in your healing, this book offers wonderful help. Cheryl's personal stories bring meaning and reality to the whole forgiveness process.

Near-death experiences

Glimpses beyond Death's Door: Gospel Insights into Near-death Experiences
Brent and Wendy Top, Granite Publishing, Orem, UT, 2005.
The authors have thoroughly researched most available near-death literature and offer striking insights and compelling quotes. They consider NDEs in the light of LDS doctrine-inspired truth and the results are edifying and intriguing.

The Message
Lance Richardson, American Family Publishing, Idaho Falls, ID, 2000.
One of the most compelling stories of a clear and impressive message from a

man who was close to death's door for years, while in a coma, crossed into the spirit world and was sent back to deliver a message.

Beyond the Veil, Volume II
Lee Nelson, Cedar Fort, Inc., Orem, UT, 1989.
A collection of 21 simple unexpected experiences of life beyond the veil, filling our need to know what happens next.

Closer to the Light
Melvin Morse, M.D. (also author of *Life after Life*), Villard Books, Random House, Inc., New York / Toronto, Canada, 1990.
Fascinating experiences related in the unbiased, innocent voices of children who have slipped beyond the veil and then returned to mortality.

There Is No Death
Sarah LaNelle Menet, Mountain Top Publishing, Philipsburg, MT, 2002.
The extraordinary true experience of Sarah LaNelle Menet. It is especially meaningful because Sarah visited the spirit world after her attempt to take her own life. Prior to this experience she had totally given up believing in God or an afterlife. Dubbed, "the most complete and extensive NDE ever recorded, Sarah not only visited the beautiful spirit world, describing the people, their dress, activities, and buildings, but also the place of torment and darkness. Gives Sarah's perspective to many questions in regard to the purpose of life.

Pre-mortal existence

The Life Before
Brent Top, Bookcraft, Inc., Salt Lake City, UT, 1988.
Perhaps this is not a book so much about death as it is about life. We lived before we received the blessing of our earthly bodies. To understand our purpose in the *here and now,* we need to know about *before* and that automatically links us to *hereafter.*

Agency and our children's choices

Rescuing Wayward Children
Larry Barkdull, Covenant Communications, Inc., American Fork, UT, 2009.
Every page in every chapter teaches with simplicity and empathy our

Savior's Perfect Plan for each of us, but particularly our beloved children who, through the gift of agency have wandered into dark and dangerous paths. Hope-filled gospel precepts to comfort and enlighten parents. (Also available in audio format.)

When a Child Wanders

Robert Millett, Deseret Book Company, Salt Lake City, UT, 1996.

Brother Millett offers his personal insight and words of comfort to parents of children lost to dangerous and wayward choices. He reminds parents of the Beloved Prodigal; the day will eventually come when we will all have opportunity to "kill the fatted calf." (Also available in audio format.)

Articles

Helpful articles abound in Church magazines. Here are a few of my favorites:

Neil F. Marriott, "Yielding Our Hearts to God," *Ensign*, Nov 2015, 30-32.

Neil shares their family's heartbreak at the death of daughter Georgia and how they had to delete the "now" from their family motto: "Things will all work out." They learned to trust God that things will work out eventually, whether here or hereafter, and that yielding our hearts to God's will is essential to our peace and happiness.

Joseph B. Wirthlin, "Sunday Will Come," *Ensign*, Nov. 2006, 28-30.

Gives beautiful assurance that, just as the Sunday of the resurrection came after the blackest Friday in history, Sunday will come for us too. "No matter our desperation, no matter our grief, Sunday will come. In this life or the next, Sunday will come."

Ezra Taft Benson, "Do Not Despair," *Ensign*, Oct. 1986, 2.

President Benson mentions the increasing numbers of suicides, and refers to D&C 45:26 where the Lord foretold that "men's heart shall fail them." This article is full of practical and inspired suggestions for overcoming discouragement and depression.

Jeffrey R. Holland, "Lessons from Liberty Jail," *Ensign*, Sept. 2009, 26-33.

He reminds us of the importance of facing inevitable suffering with love and forgiveness, and that the Spirit has a near impossible task to get through to a heart that is filled with hate or anger or vengeance or self-pity.

Donald L. Hallstrom, "Turn to the Lord," *Ensign*, May 2010, 78-80.
Shows us vividly how to avoid letting heart-breaking earthly circumstances disable us spiritually.

F. Enzio Busche, "Unleashing the Dormant Spirit," BYU Devotional, May 14, 1996. Elder Busche's talk centers on the principle that "nothing else matters unless we take the Holy Spirit as our guide and avoid being deceived." He outlines a series of excellent thoughts meant to teach us how to rejoice every day in our lives. To read this speech in PDF format, go to: speeches.byu.edu

ooo

Many of my articles can be accessed in the *Meridian Magazine* archives. They offer comfort in addition to what I could fit in this book. Go to my author page on www.meridianmagazine.com or www.ldsmag.com

C

The Life-Preserving Gift of the Scriptures

Introduction

For me personally, feasting on scriptures is not about quantity. I have found great value in selecting and repeatedly reading, writing about, even memorizing select passages that have special meaning to me. One verse that I capture—take into my heart, make part of my thinking and action and being—is worth more than many chapters skimmed but barely comprehended.

One mother asked me how I get spiritual help from the scriptures. Mainly I keep coming back to them. I search them and feast on them, especially on the days when my whole soul feels hungry. I cry with gratitude over their messages when I am in touch with my feelings . . . and still affirm that they are true when I am not. In times of spiritual desperation I grasp onto their promises like a drowning man grasps a life preserver. I've gradually been given a whole new perspective and testimony that their promises are real and true. The scriptures *are* my life preserver and my bridge back to joy.

I've found it helpful to personalize the scriptures, put my name in them, and claim them. The Lord has said they apply to each of us personally: "What I say unto one I say unto all, be of good cheer little children; for I am in your midst, and I have not forsaken you" (D&C 61:36).

Here is an example of how I personalize the scriptures: "For the Lamb which is in the midst of the throne, shall feed [me], and shall lead [me] unto living fountains of waters: and God shall wipe away all tears from [my] eyes." (See Revelation 7:17.)

I've printed lists of verses I love the most, the ones that come alive to me; many mornings I start my day by referring to some of them. The ones I've memorized I can grab onto anytime I begin sinking into the mire again; they often pull me out. My friend, Patricia, tape records her favorite helpful scriptures. She says it helps her during busy mornings or times of sickness or sadness.

Some readers of my manuscript have asked me to include a list of favorite scriptures, knowing that in the first months of grieving, a person may not have the presence of mind to look them up for themselves. Many of my favorites are sprinkled throughout this book and some are repeated here, but most of the following scriptures contain verses I have found comforting and edifying which didn't fit into the text.

Comforting Scriptures
Old Testament

"Be strong and of a good courage; be not afraid, neither be thou dismayed: for the Lord thy God is with thee withersoever thou goest." (Joshua 1:9)

"Yea, though I walk through the valley of the shadow of death, I will fear no evil: for thou art with me; thy rod and thy staff they comfort me." (Psalm 23:4)

"O Lord my God, I cried unto thee, and thou hast healed me." (Psalm 30:2)

"The Lord is nigh unto them that are of a broken heart; and saveth such as be of a contrite spirit." (Psalm 34:18)

"Many are the afflictions of the righteous: but the Lord delivereth him out of them all." (Psalm 34:19)

"God is our refuge and strength, a very present help in trouble. Therefore will not we fear . . ." (Psalm 46:1-2)

"Be still, and know that I am God." (Psalm 46:10)

"Create in me a clean heart, O God; and renew a right spirit within me. Cast me not away from thy presence; and take not thy holy spirit from me." (Psalm 51:10)

"Be merciful unto me, O God, be merciful unto me: for my soul trusteth in thee: yea, in the shadow of thy wings will I make my refuge, until these calamities be overpast." (Psalm 57:1)

"From the end of the earth will I cry unto thee, when my heart is overwhelmed: lead me to the rock that is higher than I." (Psalm 61:2)

"For thou art my hope, O Lord God: thou art my trust from my youth." (Psalm 71:5)

"My flesh and my heart faileth: but God is the strength of my heart, and my portion for ever." (Psalm 73:26)

"For he shall give his angels charge over thee, to keep thee in all thy ways." (Psalm 91:11)

"For he satisfieth the longing soul, and filleth the hungry soul with goodness." (Psalm 107:9)

"I love the Lord, because he hath heard my voice and my supplications. Because he hath inclined his ear unto me, therefore will I call upon him as long as I live. The sorrows of earth compassed me, and the pains of hell gat hold upon me: I found trouble and sorrow. Then called I upon the name of the Lord; O Lord, I beseech thee, deliver my soul. Gracious is the Lord, and righteous; yea, our God is merciful. The Lord preserveth the simple: I was brought low, and he helped me." (Psalm 116:1-6)

"They that sow in tears shall reap in joy. He that goeth forth and weepeth, bearing precious seed, shall doubtless come again with rejoicing, bringing his sheaves with him." (Psalm 126:5-6)

"Blessed be the Lord my strength . . . my goodness, and my fortress; my high tower, and my deliverer; my shield, and he in whom I trust." (Psalm 144:1-2)

"Fear thou not; for I am with thee: be not dismayed; for I am thy God: I will strengthen thee; yea, I will help thee; yea, I will uphold thee with the right hand of my righteousness." (Isaiah 41:10)

"Yea, I have loved thee with an everlasting love: therefore with lovingkindness have I drawn thee." (Jeremiah 31:3)

"A voice was heard in Ramah . . . Rahel weeping for her children refused to be comforted." And the Lord responded, "Refrain thy voice from weeping . . . for thy work shall be rewarded . . . they shall come again from the land of the enemy." (Jeremiah 31:15-16)

New Testament

"Peace I leave with you, my peace I give unto you: not as the world giveth, give I unto you. Let not your heart be troubled, neither let it be afraid." (John 14:27)

"For I am persuaded, that neither death, nor life, nor angels, nor principalities, nor powers, nor things present, nor things to come, Nor height, nor depth, nor any other creature, shall be able to separate us from the love of God, which is in Christ Jesus our Lord." (Romans 8:38-39)

"We should not trust in ourselves, but in God which raiseth the dead." (2 Corinthians 1:9)

"For ye are all the children of God by faith in Christ Jesus." (Galatians 3:26)

"God hath not given us the spirit of fear; but of power, and of love and of a sound mind." (2 Timothy 1:7)

Doctrine and Covenants

"I will encircle thee in the arms of my love." (D&C 6:20)

"For verily I say unto you, I will that ye should overcome the world; wherefore I will have compassion upon you." (D&C 64:2)

"Behold and lo, mine eyes are upon you, and the heavens and the earth are in mine hands." (D&C 67:2)

"I will go before your face. I will be on your right hand and on your left, and my Spirit shall be in your hearts, and mine angels round about you, to bear you up." (D&C 84:88)

"Verily I say unto you my friends, fear not, let your hearts be comforted; yea, rejoice evermore, and in everything give thanks." (D&C 98:1)

"Therefore, let your hearts be comforted; for all things shall work together for good to them that walk uprightly." (D&C 100:15)

"And all they who have mourned shall be comforted." (D&C 101:14)

"Wherefore, fear not even unto death; for in this world your joy is not full, but in me your joy is full." (D&C 101:36)

"If thou be cast into the deep; if the billowing surge conspire against thee; if fierce winds become thine enemy; if the heavens gather blackness, and all the elements combine to hedge up the way; and above all, if the very jaws of hell shall gape open the mouth wide after thee, know thou, my son, that all these things shall give thee experience, and shall be for thy good. The Son of Man hath descended below them all. Art thou greater than he?" (D&C 122:8)

Book of Mormon

"Whoso would hearken unto the word of God, and would hold fast unto it, they would never perish; neither could the temptations and the fiery darts of the adversary overpower them unto blindness, to lead them away to destruction." (1 Nephi 15:24)

"Thou hast suffered afflictions and much sorrow . . . Nevertheless, . . . thou knowest the greatness of God; and he shall consecrate thine afflictions for thy gain." (2 Nephi 2:1-2)

"My God hath been my support; he hath led me through mine afflictions . . . O Lord, wilt thou encircle me around in the robe of thy righteousness: . . . O Lord, I have trusted in thee, and I will trust in thee forever." (2 Nephi 4:20, 33-34)

"And now, my beloved brethren, seeing that our merciful God has given us so great knowledge concerning these things, let us remember him, and lay aside our sins, and not hang down our heads, for we are not cast off." (2 Nephi 10:20)

"And they shall be gathered into the garners, that they are not wasted. Yea, they shall not be beaten down by the storm at the last day; yea, neither shall they be harrowed up by the whirlwinds; but when the storm cometh they shall be gathered together in their place, that the storm cannot penetrate to them; yea, neither shall they be driven with fierce winds whithersoever the enemy listeth to carry them. But behold, they are in the hands of the Lord of the harvest, and they are his; and he will raise them up at the last day. Blessed be the name of our God; let us sing to his praise, yea, let us give thanks to his holy name, for he doth work righteousness forever." (Alma 26:5-8)

"He has brought them into his everlasting light, yea, into everlasting salvation; and they are encircled about with the matchless bounty of his love." (Alma 26:15)

"And thou didst hear me because of mine afflictions and my sincerity; and it is because of thy Son that thou hast been thus merciful unto me, therefore I will cry unto thee in all mine affliction, for in thee is my joy; for thou hast turned thy judgments away from me, because of thy Son." (Alma 33:11)

"As much as ye shall put your trust in God even so much ye shall be delivered out of your trials, and your troubles, and your afflictions, and ye shall be lifted up at the last day." (Alma 38:5)

"Thus we may see that the Lord is merciful unto all who will, in the sincerity of their hearts, call upon his holy name. Yea, thus we see that the gate of heaven is open unto all, even to those who will believe on the name of Jesus Christ, who is the Son of God. Yea, we see that whosoever will may lay hold upon the word of God . . . And land their souls, yea, their immortal souls, at the right hand of God in the kingdom of heaven, to sit down with Abraham, and Isaac, and with Jacob, and with all our holy fathers, to go no more out." (Helaman 3:27-30)

"Know ye not that ye are in the hands of God? Know ye not that he hath all power?" (Mormon 5:23)

If this book has been helpful, you may also enjoy Darla's other book:

What readers are saying about *Trust God No Matter What!*

"After reading Darla's book, I wish I could live next door to her, go on long walks, visit with her by my fireplace on cold winter evenings and talk about spiritual things. She is so warm and real and she speaks to my heart. Darla starts each chapter with a personal signed note, and the whole tone of her book is full of that same warmth."
—Maryn Langer, author of 12 Christian Historical Novels

"THIS IS A POWERFUL BOOK! Magnificent writing! Every paragraph rings like a trumpet call to righteous battle. Every other sentence is eminently quotable. I'm deeply impressed and mightily encouraged, as I have been going through a time of discouragement—like a dash of cold water on a fevered brow! How heartening!"
—Lorie Davis, author of *Angels Round About* and other novels.

"Darla Isackson has the courage and ability to reach deep within her own experiences and heart and emerge with truths powerful enough to change lives. She has mine. I truly believe that the spirit you feel as you walk with Darla will bring greater light to your life as well."
—Patricia Potts, author of *My Journey from Darkness to Light*

To order *Trust God No Matter What!* from:

1. *Amazon.com*
2. *Darla's website:* darlaisackson.com
3. *Deseret Book (Place a special order)*

Partial Contents of *Trust God No Matter What!*

To see the complete contents, introduction,
and sample pages, go to Darla's website

darlaisackson.com